Fashion

Fashion:
A Philosophy

Lars Svendsen

Translated by John Irons

REAKTION BOOKS

Published by Reaktion Books Ltd
33 Great Sutton Street
London EC1V 0DX, UK
www.reaktionbooks.co.uk

First published in English 2006, reprinted 2009, 2012, 2014

This book was first published in 2004 by Universitetsforlaget, Oslo, under the title *Mote: Et Filosofisk Essay* by Lars Fr. H. Svendsen

This translation has been published with the financial support of NORLA Non-fiction.

English translation by John Irons

Printed and bound in Great Britain
by Bell & Bain, Glasgow

British Library Cataloguing in Publication Data
Svendsen, Lars
Fashion: a philosophy
1. Fashion – Philosophy
I. Title
391'.001

ISBN 9 781 86189 291 1

Contents

Preface

Fashion has been one of the most influential phenomena in Western civilization since the Renaissance. It has conquered an increasing number of modern man's fields of activity and has become almost 'second nature' to us. So an understanding of fashion ought to contribute to an understanding of ourselves and the way we act. Despite this, fashion has been virtually ignored by philosophers, possibly because it was thought that this, the most superficial of all phenomena, could hardly be a worthy object of study for so 'profound' a discipline as philosophy. But if philosophy is to be a discipline that contributes to our self-understanding, and if fashion really has been – and is – as influential as I claim, it ought to be taken seriously as an object of philosophical investigation.

This book has had a long, but not difficult, birth, and much has changed *en route*. Innumerable approaches have been attempted, only to be abandoned because they proved to be blind alleys. And the final book is not what I had originally planned. It has become, not least, a more critical book than I had initially envisaged, since the subject matter forced me to adopt an increasingly critical perspective. I first began to think about writing a book on fashion five years ago, when I wrote *A Philosophy of Boredom*. In that book there was only enough space to touch briefly on the subject. The following year I published *Art*, in which the prime focus was the aestheticization of our world – and fashion is naturally an important phenomenon in that context. I felt that both books left a number of loose ends that ought to be tied together in a book on fashion. In the years that followed I gave a number of lectures on fashion, but the book I was going to write kept getting pushed aside by other assignments. Now it has finally been written.

My thanks to Ellen-Marie Forsberg, Anne Granberg, Helge Jordheim, Ingrid Sande Larsen, Thomas Sevenius Nilsen, Erik Thorstensen, Ingrid Ugelvik and Knut Olav Åmås for their comments on the text. All instances of negligence, imprecision and errors still remaining are of course my sole responsibility.

1

Introduction: A Philosophy of Fashion?

> Whatsoever sensibly exists, whatsoever represents Spirit to Spirit, is properly a Clothing, a suit or Raiment, put on for a season, and to be laid off. Thus in this one pregnant subject of CLOTHES, rightly understood, is included all that men have thought, dreamed, done, and been: the whole external Universe and what it holds is but Clothing; and the essence of all Science lies in the PHILOSOPHY OF CLOTHES.
> Thomas Carlyle[1]

> 'What's with the glasses?' she asks.
> 'Reef says it's fashionable to look like an intellectual this season.'
> Bret Easton Ellis[2]

As early as the fifteenth century fashion was considered so important in France that Charles VII was asked to establish a separate ministry of fashion.[3] Even though few would plead for such an institution nowadays, fashion has definitely not diminished in importance. Since the eighteenth century it has been increasingly democratized in the sense that it is no longer the sole preserve of a small group of affluent people. Hardly any present-day Westerner lies outside its domain. Newsagents' shelves overflow with fashion magazines, printed in bright colours on glossy paper, and fashion material fills innumerable pages of lifestyle periodicals and daily newspapers. The major fashion shows in Paris, Milan, New York and London are covered even on national TV news broadcasts. Fashion is clearly seen as important enough to warrant such a lavish degree of attention – or maybe the converse is true, maybe it is all the attention that makes fashion important. Fashion is directed at both sexes and we would seem to have abandoned the view, previously widespread, that only women are obsessed with fashion. Increasingly both young and old are pulled into its orbit. And if we widen our gaze from the realm of clothes and consider fashion as a phenomenon that encroaches on all other areas of consumption, and that its logic also encroaches on the areas of art, politics and science, it is clear that we are talking about a phenomenon that lies near the centre of the modern world.

Fashion affects the attitude of most people towards both themselves and others, though many would deny it. The denial, however, is normally contradicted by our own consumption habits – and as such it is a phenomenon that ought to be central to our attempts to understand ourselves in our historical situation. The emergence of fashion as a historical phenomenon shares a main characteristic with modernism: the break with tradition and an unceasing endeavour to reach 'the new'. Fashion, as Walter Benjamin wrote, is 'the eternal recurrence of the *new*'.[4] I would go so far as to claim that an understanding of fashion is necessary in order to gain an adequate understanding of the modern world, even though it is definitely not being asserted that fashion is the 'universal key' that is solely capable of providing such an understanding.

At the same time, fashion would seem to be one of the least important things one could imagine. In many contexts using the prefix 'fashion', as in 'fashion philosophy', is synonymous with dismissing it as something that lacks substance and gravity.[5] From the very outset fashion has had its critics. There are texts from the fourteenth century that describe how ridiculous people look when they don attire that diverges from what is strictly functional. Right up until the 1980s 'serious' studies of fashion had a tendency to express moral condemnation, maybe even contempt, for their subject matter. All this has changed, however, over the past couple of decades. This book is mostly critical of fashion, but it does not condemn it. A central ambition is to establish a more reflective relationship to fashion and as such to change our attitude towards it. This will not completely liberate us from fashion, but we can achieve a relative degree of independence from it.

This is not a history of fashion, even though the book will draw heavily on its history.[6] Nor is it a normative aesthetical investigation in the sense that I intend to assess the aesthetic value of various fashions. The aim of the book is more descriptive than normative within the area of aesthetics. Generally speaking, it is the question of fashion's relevance for the formation of identity that has preoccupied me in this investigation, although fashion can of course be analysed from many different angles. Since this is a philosophical investigation, I intend to concern myself more with the *concept* of fashion, various representations of fashion and claims as to what fashion can bring about, rather than its actual design. You could say that the subject of my investigation is the *discourse* of fashion.

The book's eight chapters may be read relatively independently of each other. They cover a wide range of topics, since fashion is related to many areas of interest, such as clothing, the body, consumption, identity and art. I intend to concentrate mainly on dress fashion, even though many other types of fashion exist. Fashion is not just a matter of clothes, but can just as well be considered as a mechanism or an ideology that applies to almost every conceivable area of the modern world, from the late medieval period onwards. This mechanism, however, has been particularly obvious within the area of clothing, so this will be centre stage in the following presentation.

'Fashion' is a notoriously difficult term to pin down, and it is extremely doubtful whether it is possible to come up with necessary and sufficient conditions for something justifiably to be called 'fashionable'. Generally speaking, we can distinguish between two main categories in our understanding of what fashion is: one can either claim that fashion refers to clothing or that fashion is a general mechanism, logic or ideology that, among other things, applies to the area of clothing.

Adam Smith, who was among the first philosophers to give fashion a central role in his anthropology, claims that fashion applies first and foremost to areas in which *taste* is a central concept. This applies in particular to clothes and furniture, but also to music, poetry and architecture.[7] In his opinion, fashion also has an influence on morals, although the influence here is considerably less.[8] Immanuel Kant provides us with a description of fashion that focuses on general changes in human lifestyles: 'All fashions are, by their very concept, mutable ways of living.'[9] But changes have taken place in human lifestyles that can scarcely be described as 'fashion', something with which Kant would agree. The Romantic poet Novalis wrote that the only 'true improvements' in human life are within the field of morals, and that all changes in our lives are 'without exception, fashions, mere changes, mere insignificant improvements'.[10] The philosopher and sociologist Georg Simmel makes a distinction in *The Philosophy of Fashion* (1904) between fashion and attire, considering fashion to be a broad social phenomenon that applies to *all* social arenas, in which clothing is merely one instance among many.[11] In his opinion, such areas as language usage and manners are also subject to fashion, although clothing is very much the centre of interest in this connection. Something similar applies to the philosopher Gilles Lipovetsky, who writes: 'Fashion is a specific form of social change, independent of any particular object; it is first and foremost a social mechanism characterized by a particularly brief time span and by more or less fanciful shifts that enable it to affect quite diverse spheres of collective life.'[12] Lipovetsky gives us here a very broad description of fashion, one which precisely emphasizes that it is a question of a general social mechanism and not just clothing. Fashion in attire is simply to be considered as one fashion phenomenon among many. It is difficult to conceive of any social phenomenon whatsoever that is not influenced by changes of fashion – whether it is body shape, car design, politics or art.

Others, however, link fashion exclusively to clothing: the art historian Anne Hollander, for example, defines 'fashion' as the entire spectrum of attractive clothes styles at any given time, including 'the *haute couture*, all forms of anti-fashion and nonfashion, and the garments and accessories of people who claim no interest in fashion.'[13] The position of the cultural historian Elisabeth Wilson lies very close to this definition: 'Fashion is dress in which the key feature is rapid and continual changing of styles. Fashion, in a sense *is* change, and in modern western societies no clothes are outside fashion.'[14] But is it the clothes themselves or a quality they have that constitutes 'fashion'? Wilson's definition is ambiguous, because it both links fashion unequivocally to clothes and to a particular quality (i.e. change). It is, however, clear here that 'change' is not a sufficient quality for describing fashion. Everything changes, but everything is not necessarily fashion. Could it be that we are searching for some other quality? One may agree with the critic and semiotician Roland Barthes that clothes are the material basis of fashion, whereas fashion itself is a cultural *system* of *meanings*.[15] But do *all* clothes serve as the material basis of such a system of meanings? That is more doubtful. It is not unreasonable to link the concept of fashion closely to clothes, but at the same time it is obvious that not all clothes can be included under 'fashion', and as such the term 'fashion' has a narrower frame of reference than the term 'clothes'. As we will see in chapter Two, fashion is not a universal phenomenon, and clothes existed long before fashions did. There is also a range of phenomena that are not clothes but which can also be described as 'fashion', and as such the term has a far wider extension than 'clothes'. It is tempting to try to define the term by considering it as a designation of a given quality (or a particular combination of qualities) that can be valid for clothes, interior design, politics, science, and other fields. The problem then is to specify accurately what this quality should be. Despite having read many studies of fashion, I have still not seen a single convincing attempt to identify such a quality. We could, of course, try to make a provisional definition of the type: something is fashion only if it functions in a socially distinctive way and is part of a system that replaces it relatively quickly with something new. However, I cannot see that such a definition would add anything important to our greater understanding of both the socially distinctive and the 'new' aspects of fashion. Furthermore, it is doubtful whether this definition would indicate necessary and sufficient conditions. It is quite conceivable that an object that is not socially distinctive and new (an old leather jacket, for example, which one has been wearing for years and is suddenly 'in') can perfectly well be described as a fashion object. There are also objects that are both socially distinctive and new (a completely new commemorative medal, for example), but which ought not to be described as fashion objects. Fashion does not actually have to introduce any new object at all; it can just as well deal with what one is *not* wearing, as when it became fashionable *not* to wear a hat. In addition, fashion applies to many different areas and it is doubtful whether a definition can be devised that captures how it functions within all these areas. There is every reason to believe that it is more effective to study the term on the basis of what Wittgenstein calls 'family resemblances'. Wittgenstein illustrates this with the concept of 'games': there is no single quality that is shared by everything we call games, but even so all games are interlinked via a complex network of similarities.[16] A consequence of such an approach to the concept of fashion is that one must close in on it via the use of examples. We can provide examples of what we would call fashion, as well as examples of what we would not call fashion, but we neither can nor may come up with a definition with necessary and sufficient conditions. So there will be considerable use of examples in this book, and we will have to see to what extent it is possible to extract any more general points on the basis of these examples.

Fashions naturally also exist among academics and intellectuals. They have to do with which subjects are 'in' and which are 'out', which approaches are 'sexy' and which are not. It would be naïve to believe that all this is governed by completely rational considerations, since it is just as much a question of constantly shifting taste. There is really no big difference between clothes and philosophy in this respect, although philosophers react more slowly than those in the world of fashionwear: it is not expected of every philosopher that he or she should present a completely new collection of opinions each season. The idea that philosophy, among other things, is a fashion-controlled process can seem somewhat objectionable to philosophers, who like to believe that exclusively rational choices underlie what themes and approaches they employ. Some philosophers, indeed, reacted strongly to a formulation I suggested in an earlier book:

> There are few clear refutations in the history of philosophy. When philosophical revolutions take place, for example with Descartes and Kant, it is not because their predecessors have been incontestably refuted, but

> rather because many philosophers are tired of traditional philosophy and feel it is just ticking over, so that something new is called for.[17]

To say that philosophy does not change solely for rational reasons, but quite often for the sake of change itself, is to concede that philosophy too, at least partially, is subject to fashion. This, though, is a description that challenges the ambition of modern philosophy to attain an absolutely rational self-determination.

The philosopher Hans-Georg Gadamer claims that fashion regulates only those things that could just as easily have been completely different.[18] Fashion, then, should be seen as something completely random without any deeper grounding – a groundless surface. But fashion does not restrict itself to only ruling over such 'unimportant' things as clothes – it also affects art and science. Elsewhere, Gadamer writes: 'Even in the praxis of scientific work there is such a thing as "fashion". We know what enormous power and overwhelming force fashion represents. It is only that the word "fashion" sounds so terribly bad in connection with science for self-evidently it is our claim that science is superior to that which merely promotes fashion.'[19] Simmel shares this view, maintaining that such phenomena as science and religiosity are too important to be subject to 'a complete lack of objectiveness in the development of fashion'.[20] The question is if we really can live up to such an ambition and rise above the demands of fashion. A central point of Gadamer's hermeneutics is that every attempt to understand something, every scientific or non-scientific investigation, must of necessity be linked to a historically conditioned hermeneutic situation. To what extent is our hermeneutic situation influenced by the logic of fashion? Why should one try to rise above fashion in the way Gadamer maintains? Will the person who follows fashion be out of harmony with his age

– and does this not have a value in itself? It is perhaps to this that Hegel is alluding when he claims that it is 'folly' to resist fashion.[21]

Fashion cannot at any rate be said to be a fashionable theme in philosophy. Even in broadly based philosophical works that deal with the genesis of the modern self, such as Charles Taylor's *Sources of the Self*, fashion is passed over in silence.[22] Traditionally, fashion is not considered a satisfactory object of study and the field has not gained the same recognition as, for example, the visual arts and architecture. The position has changed to a certain degree in recent years with a stream of academic publications on fashion. With a few exceptions, however, these have not been written by philosophers. If we look back through the history of philosophy, the results are also meagre. Even Nietzsche avoids the theme to a great extent. The list of those who have actually devoted a certain amount of attention to fashion includes Adam Smith, Immanuel Kant, G.W.F. Hegel, Walter Benjamin and Theodor W. Adorno. There are also scattered remarks by other thinkers, but surprisingly little material to draw on in the philosophical tradition. I know of only two philosophers who have written whole books about fashion: Georg Simmel and Gilles Lipovetsky (although sociologists will presumably claim that Simmel is really 'their' man). It goes a little against the nature of philosophy to write about fashion. Plato draws the distinction between reality itself on the one hand and its appearances on the other, between depth and surface. And fashion is surface through and through. It is, by the way, also possible to notice a certain scepticism about clothes as early as Plato, who links clothes to beauty, but a beauty of a somewhat fraudulent nature.[23] That fashion has been neglected by philosophy would seem to stem from a conception that the phenomenon itself is too superficial to merit serious investigation. In general, philosophers have not been highly fashion-conscious, either. Once more an exception is Kant, who was known as 'the elegant Master of Arts' and who tripped around in shoes with silver buckles and wore fine silk shirts. As Kant himself expressed it: 'It is always better [. . .] to be a fool in fashion than a fool out of fashion.'[24]

To write a philosophy of fashion is to assume a task that has basically been ridiculed in imaginative writing – more precisely in Thomas Carlyle's novel *Sartor Resartus* (1833–4). When Carlyle began work on the book, he wrote in his diary: 'I am going to write – Nonsense. It is on "Clothes". Heaven be my comforter!'[25] The book pokes fun at fashion, not least its philosophy. The main character is Diogenes Teufelsdröckh ('devil's shit'), who has decided to investigate 'the moral, political, even religious Influences of Clothes'.[26] He makes clothes the basis of everything in human existence, claiming that this existence is fundamentally best understood through clothes: 'Thus in this one pregnant subject of CLOTHES, rightly understood, is included all that men have thought, dreamed, done, and been: the whole external Universe and what it holds is but Clothing; and the essence of all Science lies in the PHILOSOPHY OF CLOTHES.'[27] Naturally, clothes are unable to bear such a burden. It then turns out that it is not the actual items of clothing that interest Teufelsdröckh, rather their meaning. He underlines that the original purpose of clothing was neither warmth nor decency but ornamentation.[28] Teufelsdröckh wants to use clothes in order to read the world. This is the important thing for a philosophical investigation of fashion: the meaning of fashion. It must also be stressed that the widespread conception of *Sartor Resartus* as a rejection of fashion can only partially be said to be true. Rather than being an attack on fashion as such, Carlyle wishes to defend human authenticity – that the inner is to correspond to the outer, and that one's outer self ought to be the expression of a genuine spirituality. To a great extent Carlyle considered *Sartor Resartus* a joke, and the book is undeniably amusing, but even so it is also one of the most perceptive books ever written about fashion: Carlyle realizes that clothes are of crucial importance for the constitution of the human self.

As Simmel has emphasized in his *Philosophy of Fashion*, there is a link between fashion and identity. It is this track I have sought to follow in the present book. Clothes are a vital part of the social construction of the self. Identity is no longer provided by a tradition, but it is just as much something we have to choose by virtue of the fact that we are consumers. Fashion is not just about class differentiation, as has been claimed in classic sociological analyses from Veblen to Bourdieu, but just as much about expressing one's individuality. Clothing is part of the individual, not something external in relation to personal identity. The philosopher and writer Hélène Cixous emphasizes, for example, that clothes are not primarily a shield for the body but function rather as an extension of it.[29] All of us have to express in some way who we are via our visual appearance. Of neces-sity this expression will be in a dialogue with fashion and the increasingly rapid cycles of fashion indicate a more complex conception of the self, because the self becomes more transient.

What is it like to live in a world with fashion as a principle? We become chronically stimulated by a steady stream of 'new' phenomena and products, but we also become bored more quickly to a corresponding extent. In Jay McInerney's novel *Model Behaviour* it is said that we are 'in the sphere of fashion, where breathless enthusiasm sings in harmony with poisonous boredom'.[30] We are liberated from a series of traditional connections, but become slaves of new institutions. We try harder and harder to express our own individuality, but paradoxically do so in a way that very often merely becomes the expression of an abstract impersonality.

Naturally, there are plenty who fall outside the domain of fashion but in our part of the world, and at this point in history, it is practically impossible to stay outside the sphere of fashion. Even the poorest in the Western world are incorporated into the field of fashion by being aware that they cannot participate to any great extent. To be excluded from the game, and aware of being excluded, is to be within its sphere. All those who read this book are citizens of the world of fashion.

2

The Principle of Fashion: The New

Make it new!
Ezra Pound[1]

A new idea.
A new look.
A new sex.
A new pair of underwear.
Andy Warhol[2]

Fashion is not universal. It is not a phenomenon that exists everywhere and at all times. Its roots are neither in human nature nor in group mechanisms in general. Since it first arose in one society, it has induced an ever-increasing number of other societies and social areas into following its logic.

It is normally claimed that fashion in clothes has its origins in the late medieval period, possibly early in the Renaissance, perhaps in connection with the growth of mercantile capitalism. The usual argument is that one cannot talk about fashion in Greek and Roman antiquity in the sense we do today because there was no individual aesthetic autonomy in the choice of clothing – even though there were certain possibilities for variation. European clothing had changed relatively little from the Roman Age to the fourteenth century. Although there had of course been variations in clothing as regards materials and details, to all intents and purposes the *form* of clothes remained unaltered. Broadly speaking, rich and poor wore clothing of similar form, although rich people had their clothes made of more expensive materials and decorated themselves with ornaments. The impulse to decorate oneself is by no means a recent phenomenon in human history, but what people decorated themselves with in the pre-modern world had nothing to do with fashion. The Vikings, for example, were very preoccupied with their appearance, and it was usual to have, among other things, a comb hanging from a belt that also included symbols of rank – but there were no Viking fashions. Pre-modern societies are conservative. People in such societies can wear simple or sophisticated decorations and can be enormously preoccupied with aesthetical phenomena, but it is a recurring characteristic that such as hairstyles, clothes and jewellery remain more or less unaltered for generations. The Romans of antiquity were vain, with both men and women using make-up and perfume, and with their hair dyed and curled if they did not use a wig. But such styles were also long-lasting. A style from one country might occasionally become popular in another, leading to a sudden change of style – as when the Greeks began to remove their beards in order to resemble Alexander the Great. Such a change of style, however, does not need to be referred to as a *fashion*, for the Greeks subsequently retained their shaven cheeks and chins. What happened was that one long-lasting aesthetic norm was replaced by another, without further changes apparently having been wished for or even considered. In order to be able to talk of 'fashion' it is not sufficient for a change to take place on rare occasions. It only becomes a fashion when this change is sought for its own sake and takes place relatively frequently.

As mentioned, the origin of fashion is usually linked to the emergence of mercantile capitalism in the late medieval period. Europe was then experiencing considerable economic development, and the economic changes created the basis for relatively swift cultural changes. It was here that changes in people's clothing first acquired a particular logic: change was no longer rare or random, but was rather cultivated for its own sake. Clothes changed their basic shapes rapidly, with changes in superficial details taking place even faster. They also began to resemble modern attire by being adapted to the individual person, with the cut being changed over time without any reason apparent other than the change itself. Around the mid-fifteenth century creative cuts, new colours and textures began to emerge, with variations in width across the shoulders and the chest, the length of clothing, the design of hats and shoes, and other changes. This tendency further intensified, gaining perhaps its most extreme form of expression in the constantly increasing divergences from the actual contours of the body evident in the sixteenth century. Change in clothes became a source of pleasure in itself. Naturally for centuries this conscious change of styles was accessible to only the few, the rich, but it gradually spread with the emergence of the bourgeoisie, together with concurrent desire to be 'in fashion'.

Even though it can be claimed that fashion began around 1350, it would be more correct to say that fashion in its modern sense – with quick changes and a constant challenge to the individual to keep abreast of the age – did not become a real force until the eighteenth century. The bourgeoisie that emerged at this time, competing with the feudal aristocracy for power, used clothes to signal their social status. In the 1770s and '80s the first fashion magazines made their appearance, such as the English *Lady's Magazine* (1770) and the German *Journal des Luxus und der Moden* (1786). (Fashion magazines explicitly for a male public, however, were not published until the 1920s.)[3] Such magazines doubtless served to increase the circulation speed of fashion, since information about what was 'in' and 'out' was spread far faster and to more people than before.

The growth of fashion is one of the most decisive events in world history, because it indicates the direction of modernity.

There is in fashion a vital trait of modernity: the abolition of traditions. Nietzsche emphasizes fashion as a characteristic of the modern because it is an indication of emancipation from, among other things, authorities.[4] But there also lies in fashion an element that modernity would not have wished to acknowledge. Fashion is irrational. It consists of change for the sake of change, whereas the self-image of modernity consisted in there being a change that led towards increasingly rational self-determination.

Modernization consists of a dual movement: emancipation always involves the introduction of a form of coercion, since the opening of one form of self-realization always closes another. According to Roland Barthes: 'Every new Fashion is a refusal to inherit, a subversion against the oppression of the preceding Fashion.'[5] Seen in this way, an emancipation lies in the new fashion, as one is liberated from the old one. The problem is that the one suppression is replaced by another, as one is immediately subject to the tyranny of the new fashion. Modernity liberated us from tradition, but it made us slaves of a new imperative, one precisely formulated by Arthur Rimbaud towards the end of *Une saison en enfer*: 'We have to be utterly modern.'[6]

The idea of 'the new' is relatively new. Medieval people, for example, did not think in such terms. Some clarification is perhaps called for at this point. Naturally, people have always been aware of certain things being newer than others, and there are examples of the use of the Latin expression *modernus* ('new' or 'recent', the basis of the concept 'modernity') all the way back to the sixth century, when it was used to distinguish between a heathen age and a new Christian era. It was, however, not until much later that the distinction between 'new' and 'old' attained widespread use. An indication that a new understanding of time and history was emerging is that people became aware of the fact that anachronisms existed. In paintings from the Middle Ages we see, for example, biblical figures being depicted in medieval attire. The Holy Family could be depicted wearing clothes that would have suited an Italian merchant's family. There does not seem to have been any clear awareness of the fact that the figures depicted had used 'old' clothes, while they had been depicted with 'new' clothes. The conception of 'the new' did not become widespread until the advent of the Enlightenment during the eighteenth century. The philosopher Gianni Vattimo points out that modernity is an era in which being modern becomes a value in itself or, rather, where being modern becomes the fundamental value to which all others are referred.[7] More precisely, being 'modern' becomes synonymous with being 'new'. Modern man has a 'pro-neo' turn of mind.

Practically all fashion theorists stress 'the new' – with a steady stream of 'new' objects replacing those that were 'new' but have now become 'old' – as a basic characteristic of fashion. I am aware of only one writer who claims the opposite, the architect Adolf Loos. Paradoxically enough, Loos considers something really modern only if it has duration: only objects that are fashionable over a lengthy period of time deserve the term 'fashion'.[8] If something goes out of fashion after just one season, it has, according to Loos, only pretended to be modern, without actually being so. Loos also believes that objects without decoration would be far more aesthetically durable than those that are richly ornamented, and that men's fashion ought therefore to replace women's fashion.[9] He inscribes fashion in a concept of progress seen as an approach towards an increasingly pure form of expression, and fashion becomes complete when it has done away with all ornamentation and change. He also claims that the person who differs *least* from everyone else will be the most fashionable.[10] Loos's understanding of the concept of fashion, however, is so idiosyncratic that I do not intend to take further account of it.

Kant is perhaps the first fashion theorist of any real stature to emphasize *the new* as an essential characteristic of fashion: 'Novelty makes fashion alluring.'[11] While earlier theorists had linked fashion to beauty, Kant emphasizes that it does not have to have anything to do with beauty at all but that, on the contrary, it 'degenerate(s) into something fantastic and even detestable', since it is more a question of competition than a matter of taste.[12]

In this respect Kant is more 'modern' than Charles Baudelaire, who linked fashion to a striving towards beauty. Baudelaire describes every single fashion as a symptom of 'a new and more or less happy effort in the direction of Beauty, some kind of approximation to an ideal for which the restless human mind feels a constant, titillating hunger'.[13] It can be claimed that Baudelaire, despite his fascination with fashion, only takes half a step out into it. He wants 'to extract from fashion whatever element it may contain of poetry within history, to distil the eternal from the transitory'.[14] For Baudelaire, beauty is a question of finding a synthesis of the eternal and the temporal:

> Beauty is made up of an eternal, invariable element, whose quantity it is excessively difficult to determine, and of a relative, circumstantial element, which will be, if you like, whether severally or all at once, the age, its fashions, its morals, its emotions. Without this second element, which might be described as the amusing, enticing, appetizing icing on the divine cake, the first element would be beyond our powers of digestion or appreciation, neither adapted nor suitable to human nature. I defy anyone to point to a single scrap of beauty which does not contain these two elements.[15]

It was basically this wager that Stéphane Mallarmé took up. Mallarmé radicalized Baudelaire's standpoint, and did not seek any synthesis of the eternal and the temporal. For him, the transient and the immediate are sufficient. Between

September and December 1874 Mallarmé was editor of a fashion magazine, *La Dernière Mode*, in which, under diverse pseudonyms, he wrote absolutely all the editorial material, including articles advising on dresses, hats and other items.[16] Beauty in fashion was not to find an attraction in something eternal, and not at all in any functionality, but in sheer temporality. For modern aesthetics, beauty lies in the temporal, in the transient that is absolutely contemporaneous.

Gradually beauty drops out as a central aesthetic norm, and the insistence on something being new becomes the most crucial factor: the logic of fashion has outdone all other aesthetic conditions. This is particularly obvious in the visual arts and similar forms of expression. The poet Paul Valéry was critical of this tendency: 'The exclusive taste for newness shows the degeneration of the critical faculty, for nothing is easier than assessing the newness of a work.'[17] Roland Barthes states this more soberly: 'Our evaluation of the world no longer depends [. . .] on the opposition between *noble* and *base* but on that between Old and New.'[18]

The insistence on originality was the mantra of the artistic avant-garde.[19] At the same time it is clear that every presumptively original utterance is encapsulated in an overwhelmingly larger context of repetition. When an artist or creator of fashion does something new, it will be found (assuming one has done one's homework in the history of art and fashion) that the '*underlying condition of the original*' is the 'ever-present reality of the copy', as the art theorist Rosalind Krauss points out.[20] It is, however, possible to claim that the cultivation of novelty by the avant-garde was fuelled by the aim of creating the definitively new that could not be surpassed by anything even newer, and that as such it did not completely embrace the logic of fashion. This was, for example, the ambition of Mark Rothko, who stated in the early 1950s that he and the other Abstract Expressionists had set a new standard for art that would apply for the next thousand years.[21] In actual fact it lasted no more than a decade, even though it was an extraordinary decade. Fashion would basically seem never to have been subject to this illusion and has, if anything, always foreseen that everything new will soon be surpassed by something even newer.

Both fashion and modern art – possibly because art is subject to the logic of fashion – have been governed by an 'urge to innovate'.[22] While the pre-modern artist was subject to a demand to remain within the framework of tradition, the modern artist has been subject to a demand to exceed such frameworks – and always to create something *new*. The constant break with what has gone before is not freely chosen – it is much more a strict convention of modern art. According to the philosopher Boris Groys: 'The striving for the new manifests the reality of our culture precisely when it is freed of all ideological motives and justifications, and the difference between true, authentic innovation and untrue, non-authentic innovation no longer applies.'[23] It is sufficient that something is new. The new has become self-justifying – it does not need any reference to a concept of progress or something similar.

A fashion object does not *in principle* need any particular qualities apart from being new.[24] The principle of fashion is to create an ever-increasing velocity, to make an object superfluous as fast as possible, in order to let a new one have a chance. Seen in this light, the Gap chain of clothes shops is exemplary, as it replaces its product line every eight weeks![25] Fashion is irrational in the sense that it seeks change for the sake of change, not in order to 'improve' the object, for example by making it more functional. It seeks superficial changes that in reality have no other assignment than to make the object superfluous on the basis of non-essential qualities, such as the number of buttons on a suit jacket or the famous skirt length. Why do skirts become shorter? Because they have been long. Why do they become long? Because they have been short. The same applies to all other objects of fashion. Fashion is not 'more profound' than calling for change for the sake of change.

Where do changes in fashion come from? It is always tempting to try to find a correspondence between fashion trends and those of outside society – and there will of course be points of contact since fashion is an important part of this society, but fashions are created first and foremost on the basis of previous fashions, and not as a 'comment on society', or the like. If skirts are longer for a season, it is not because society has become more puritanical, but because they have been shorter. In short: fashion develops more on the basis of internal conditions than a dialogue with the political developments in society.[26] Nor can it be understood as an attempt to reach a timeless ideal. In his early writings, the sociologist Jean Baudrillard seems to assume a given ideal of beauty that fashion falls short of, as when he asserts that 'really beautiful, definitively beautiful clothes would put an end to fashion'.[27] Later, however, he makes fashion the overriding principle to which all ideals of beauty are also subject. Fashion does not have any *telos*, any final purpose, in the sense of striving for a state of perfection, a kind of highest incarnation that will make all future developments superfluous. The aim of fashion is rather to be potentially endless, that is it creates new forms and constellations *ad infinitum*.

On the other hand, one can ask to what extent anything new still exists. Given the number of fashion shows each year, it is obvious that there is little time for developing new ideas. It would appear to be more natural to create variations on previous fashions. One can talk about certain general trends in fashion over lengthy periods of time, such as how the cut of clothes has been made simpler and more skin has become visible over the past centuries, but there are major variations within these periods. Following the straight lines and almost ascetic, modernist style of the 1920s and '30s, Christian Dior's 'New Look', which he introduced after the Second World War, required a profusion of material and displayed a return to a more 'bourgeois' fashion that reflected more traditional concepts of gender. The style seemed to be a radical innovation, but in a certain sense it was a retro-fashion. As a couturier, Dior contributed greatly to increasing the tempo of fashion by surprising people with constantly new, unexpected creations each season, at a time when fashion developed far more slowly than today.

Time and space have become ever more compressed. Objective time and objective space have, of course, the same quantitative properties as before, but *experienced time* and *experienced space* have 'shrunk'. This leads to a change in the temporality of fashion. Whereas fashion formerly could seem to have a more linear temporality, it has to an increasing extent now acquired a cyclic temporality. Here it should be pointed out that there has always been a cyclic element in fashion: as early as the fifteenth century styles from the previous were beginning to be repeated.[28] Early in the history of fashion, however, a cycle lasted considerably longer than later on, and fashion can be said to have had a general forward movement. Today, however, it seems to be completely taken up with recycling itself. The new freedom of fashion over the past decades has not so much been used to create new forms as to play with older forms.[29] Nowadays, it is scarcely justifiable to claim that any fashion is historically more advanced than any other one. All fashions have been placed on an equal footing.

Fashion exists in an interaction between forgetting and remembering, in which it still remembers its past by recycling it, but at the same time forgets that the past is exactly that. And the faster fashion evolves, one would presume, the faster it will forget. As Milan Kundera wrote: 'The degree of slowness is directly proportional to the intensity of memory; the degree of speed is directly proportional to the intensity of forgetting.'[30] But is this true? Has today's fashion – precisely because of its extreme speed – become one with far too good a memory?

Roland Barthes claimed in his major book on fashion that it is a discourse that rejects the possibility of a dialogue with its own past.[31] Since Barthes' book appeared in 1967, however, fashion has to an increasing extent consisted of precisely such a dialogue with its own past, which at the moment is constantly being retrieved as a substitute for the new.

The nature of fashion is to be transient. There is a central insistence on radical innovation, a constant hunt for originality. Fashion is only fashion insofar as it is capable of moving forwards. Fashion moves in cycles, where a cycle is the space of time from when a fashion is introduced to when it is replaced by a new one, and the principle of fashion is to make the cycle – the space of time – as short as possible, so as to create the maximum number of successive fashions. The ideal fashion, seen in this way, would only last a moment before it was replaced by a new one. In that sense, fashion has come closer and closer to a realization of its essence, since its cycles have become shorter and shorter, from having lasted a decade in the nineteenth century to lasting only a season from the 1970s onwards. There is broad agreement that the cycles of fashion have accelerated rapidly since the nineteenth century, especially over the last fifty years. Naturally, no one is able to create radically new styles at such a rate, and a recycling of former styles has become the norm in fashion. The *haute couture* of the 1970s did not essentially break any new ground, but was rather a further development of the 1960s, although with a greater emphasis on 'naturalness'. The fashions of the 1980s quite explicitly quoted and recycled, but without the more nostalgic tone of the 1970s. By the time we reach the 1990s it is hard to see anything other than an endless series of recyclings – albeit in spectacular variants. This recycling is rarely completely pure, in the sense that we are looking at direct copies of former items of clothing. It is usually rather more a question of dissimilar constellations of elements from former fashions, or more extreme versions of specific styles. It is just as much a question of recycling when contemporary designers 'install' themselves in a position at the end of fashion history and no longer believe in a further forward movement, so that the only remaining strategy is to recreate the styles of former times in various variants. And the link to their historical origins becomes increasingly weak. Fashion decontextualizes and re-contextualizes, and the fashion items that are appropriated from other traditions no longer have any fixed origin.[32]

Recycling has also speeded up, and today we are in a situation where practically speaking all styles overlap each other as regards time. The temporal distance between the 'new' and the recycled fashion has become less and less until it finally disappeared. Martin Margiela explicitly broke the rules of fashion when he repeated his earlier creations in new collections and in so doing repudiated the demand that he should be 'new'. This only revealed, however, that Margiela had realized the impossibility of being completely 'new' each season. He has worked with this idea in various ways: in 1997, for example, he made 'new' clothes out of old collections (a outfit from each of the eighteen collections he had produced) and then made then 'old' again by sprinkling them with fertilizing agents and spraying them with bacteria and mould and yeast fungi before putting them on show at Museum Boijmans van Beuningen in Rotterdam.

If Walter Benjamin was right in claiming that fashion is 'the eternal recurrence of the *new*',[33] it would be hard to imagine anything more untimely than fashion. The category 'the new' seems, despite everything, to belong to the past. Rather than an eternal recurrence of the new, an eternal recurrence of the same would seem to be the rule. Fashion no longer seems to contain any surprises for us. New collections are shown to the press almost a year in advance and they follow well-worn tracks. It does not seem particularly appropriate at all to talk about 'fashion cycles' any more, since a cycle presumes that something is 'in fashion' before it goes 'out of fashion'. Since the early 1990s the recycling process has reached such a speed that something hardly has time to go out of fashion before it is back in fashion again. The result is that contemporary fashion is characterized by a general contemporaneity of all styles. With the ever-increasing speed of recycling we have come to a point where fashion – by realizing its potential to the full – has done away with its own logic.

Fashion used to follow a modernist norm, in that a new fashion was to replace all previous ones and make them superfluous. The traditional logic of fashion is a *logic of replacement*. For the last ten years, however, fashion has been defined by a *logic of supplementation*, by which all trends are recyclable and a new fashion hardly aims at replacing all those that have gone before, but rather contents itself with supplementing them.[34] The logic of replacement has itself been replaced by that of supplementation (or one of accumulation, if you prefer), in which the mechanism that promises that the new will replace the old is no longer operative. Instead, the old and the new – or rather, perhaps, the old and the old – exist side by side. As Andy Warhol established for art: 'There's room for everybody.'[35] The *modus operandi* of fashion has changed. Traditionally, fashion requires a steady stream of new objects that will soon become superfluous. The aim of fashion is the ceaseless continuation of a system that replaces the already existing one with something new, without any justification other than that the new is preferable to what already exists. Fashion does not have any *ultimate goal* except an eternal realization and radicalization of its own logic. But when this logic became sufficiently radicalized, it was transformed from one of replacement to one of supplement. The problem with such a logic of supplementation is that it does not create a sufficiently high degree of superfluity.

In presentations of utopias, fashion is normally absent. We can already see this in Thomas More's *Utopia*, where everyone wears the same type of functional clothes that have not been dyed and have not changed their form for centuries.[36] More also stresses that all clothes are used until they wear out.[37] Totalitarian regimes have also had a tendency to insist that all citizens of the state wear uniforms. The Mao outfit is a typical example. Boris Groys describes fashion as anti-utopian and anti-authoritarian because its constant change undermines the possibility of there being universal truths that would be able to determine the future.[38] One could say that in this way the anti-authoritarian tendency results from the anti-utopian dimension of fashion, although fashion is, on the other hand, perhaps the most totalitarian phenomenon of all in the modern world, since it has imposed its own logic onto practically all areas and thus become all-encompassing. Fashion has conquered most areas, but lost itself in the process. It is everywhere, but that also means that it is nowhere. Can something like fashion exist without there being a dominant style or, at least, a highly restricted number of dominant styles? No style has completely dominated the field of fashion since the 1960s. What we have seen since is an increasing polymorphism of the field. An absolutely fashionable style does not have to be adopted by the majority of a community or a culture. On the contrary, too great a spread of fashion indicates that something is on the way out. A genuinely fashionable style must rather be one adopted by a minority that is *on its way* to becoming that of the majority, or at least that of a large number of people. In that sense, fashion never *is* – it is always in a state of *becoming*. What we have today is not in such a state of becoming; it is, if anything, a constant reserve of recyclable styles, with none basically more 'in fashion' than the others.

Not only have a number of couturiers recycled old fashions in new collections, some have gone a step further by recycling their own former creations in new collections. Martin Margiela was perhaps the first, but Diane von Furstenberg made the point quite explicitly in 2001 when she made an exact reproduction of a dress she had launched in 1972, relaunching it with precisely the same advertisement that she had used at its first appearance. Dolce & Gabbana and Prada have opened shops that sell clothes from former collections. Vivienne Westwood produces items of clothing from old productions on commission. Manolo Blahnik has brought old shoe collections into production, and Fendi has done the same with his bags. If fashion has basically become recycling, one might just as well recycle oneself. It is, however, difficult to imagine a more flagrant break with the basic idea of fashion, since formerly it always was a question of producing something *new*.

Benjamin asked if fashion dies because it fails to maintain velocity.[39] But is this death not rather due to the fact that fashion had reached a critical speed that changed its entire logic?

3

The Origins and Spread of Fashion

'Pray how many suits does she wear out in a year?'
'Oh, dear Sir! A fine lady's clothes are not old by being worn but by being seen.'
Richard Steele[1]

Things must change
We must rearrange them
Or we'll have to estrange them.
All that I'm saying
A game's not worth playing
Over and over again.
Depeche Mode[2]

Why did fashion become so attractive? What was it about fashion that attracted so many people into its sphere? In this chapter we will look more closely at a number of theories as to how and why fashion develops the way it does.[3] Various versions of the so-called 'trickle-down' theory will be central, as this is the actual basic model in most accounts of the development of fashion, but we will also see that this theory has become steadily less tenable as fashion has continued to develop.

The growth of fashion can be seen as a result of the attempt to combat it. In medieval Europe the church and state cooperated on combating luxury. Contact with the east, notably during the crusades, had brought choice fabrics and precious stones to Europe. As people began to compete in displays of wealth, the church and state looked on this trend with some scepticism and wished to control it. Some of the most important regulations introduced at this time were the sumptuary laws, which were designed not least with clothing in mind. The term 'sumptuary' derives from the Latin *sumptuarius* ('relating to expense', 'luxury'). These laws were in force, broadly speaking, from the thirteenth century to the seventeenth. Particular stipulations were developed for use in relation to rank, where certain articles of clothing and other objects were reserved for certain social classes. It was forbidden for lower classes to acquire such apparel, even though they might be able to afford them. This was by no means the first time such laws had existed. In ancient Egypt, for example, only the upper classes were allowed to wear sandals, and both the Greeks and the Romans had rules regarding who was allowed to wear what. The toga was reserved for Roman citizens: whoever was not a Roman citizen had no right to wear a toga, and anyone deprived of his citizenship had to stop wearing one. In the Middle Ages, however, such rules were considerably more specific and comprehensive. Mercantile capitalism had created a more 'fluid' society with a certain social mobility, with laws also being introduced to maintain class differences.[4] Just as important, however, was the wish to preserve morals, because luxury items were thought to corrupt. Lavish clothing was a clear indication of vanity, something that was a serious sin in itself. The sumptuary laws were, of course, constantly being broken – it almost seemed as if the ban made the commodities even more attractive – which should hardly surprise anyone. These laws served precisely to strengthen the role of clothes as an important social marker as they created relatively clear criteria for the social status of various objects. With the increasing weakening of class divisions and greater social mobility, however, the battle to maintain such rules was lost. Admittedly certain bans were introduced later (against women wearing trousers, for example), but these were not targeted against social classes but against all human beings, or everyone of a single gender. There have also been certain political bans, as when the English occupying power forbade the Scots to wear kilts, or the recent French ban against the use of religious symbols in schools – something that was effectively a ban against the use of the *hijab*.

'Common' people (i.e. the working class) were not drawn into the domain of fashion until the nineteenth century. Until then they had been excluded for economic reasons, but the rapid expansion of mass production, not least the introduction of sewing machines and knitting machines, enabled large quantities of clothes of relatively complex shapes, which had previously been the privilege of hand-sewing, to be produced. This opened up completely new possibilities for mass consumption. Previously clothing had been extremely valuable.[5] The most valuable thing a person from the lower classes could hope to inherit could well be an item of clothing. Normally people did not have more than one set of clothes. This changed dramatically with the expansion of mass production, which made more clothing readily accessible to more people. This 'democratization' of fashion did not mean that all distinctions were erased, rather that almost everybody was incorporated into the social interplay of fashion. While the struggle to look distinguished had formerly been reserved for the highest echelons of society, mass production made it possible for the lower classes to take part as well. Since then this tendency has only increased.

In the nineteenth century mass production and mass consumption mushroomed. Since then mass consumption has to an increasing extent assumed the form of symbol consumption, that is it takes place so as to bring about an identification with what the consumption item *stands for*. Mass-produced items constitute not least a resource for members of the masses to raise themselves above their fellows. Since the rest have the same interest, we get a cumulative tendency in mass consumption that will in future spiral off at increasing velocity (naturally, subject to the limitations the present economic situation might impose). The desire for symbolically potent consumer items then becomes a self-fuelling mechanism that is both the cause and a consequence of social inequality. This is normally presented as the result of a so-called 'trickle-down' effect, where innovation takes place at a higher level and then spreads downwards because the lower social classes strive to move upwards, which results in their always being one step behind.[6]

The early rudiments of such a theory are to be found as early as Adam Smith in *The Theory of Moral Sentiments* (1759):

> It is from our disposition to admire, and consequently to imitate, the rich and the great, that they are enabled to set, or to lead what is called the fashion. Their dress is the fashionable dress; the language of their conversation, the fashionable style; their air and deportment, the fashionable behaviour. Even their vices and follies are fashionable; and the greater part of men are proud to imitate and resemble them in the very qualities which dishonour and disgrace them.[7]

A little later we find a related theory in Kant's *Anthropology from a Pragmatic Point of View*, possibly influenced by Smith's work, which was translated into German in 1770:

> It is a natural inclination of man to compare his behaviour to that of a more important person (the child compares itself to grown-ups, and the lowly compares himself to the aristocrat) in order to imitate the other person's ways. A law of such imitation, which aims at not appearing less important than others, especially when no regard is paid to gaining any profit

> from it, is called fashion. Therefore it belongs under the title of vanity, because in its intention there is no inner value; at the same time, it belongs also under the title of folly, because in fashion there is still a compulsion to subject oneself slavishly to the mere example which many in society project to us.[8]

Kant emphasizes the delay, that fashion is used 'by the lower ranks after those at court have discarded it'. This is the actual basic model that will come to dominate theories about fashion right up until our own age.

Most later 'trickle-down' theories have probably been inspired more by the philosopher Herbert Spencer than by Kant. Spencer traces the origins of fashion back to emblems and other things that symbolize status, pointing out that such distinguishing characteristics have a tendency to spread to more than those who, strictly speaking, are entitled to them.[9] This spread is caused by the lower classes having a tendency to try to raise themselves to the level of the higher classes by donning their characteristics. Spencer, however, expects fashion to disappear in the long term with the increasing democratization of society. It could, though, be argued against Spencer that precisely the opposite will be the result of such a 'democratic levelling', that the breaking down of social hierarchies will make it even more important for the individual to be able to accentuate himself with the aid of fashion – and is that not exactly what has happened?

Spencer has an optimistic view of the future, viewing modernity as a forward motion towards an ever more rational society. The sociologist Thorstein Veblen does not share this view, considering modernity to a great extent to be an irrational orgy of consumption. Veblen's condemnation of modern consumption sometimes rushes on unabated, and Jorge Luis Borges claims that he thought Veblen's book on 'the leisure class' was a satire when he read it for the first time.[10]

According to Veblen: 'This requirement of novelty is the underlying principle of the whole difficult and interesting domain of fashion. Fashion does not demand continual flux and change simply because that way of doing is foolish; flux and change and novelty are demanded by the central principle of dress – conspicuous waste.'[11] Veblen states that it is not sufficient to have money and power in order to achieve social standing: it also has to be visible.[12] It is a question of *showing* what social status one has, for example via *conspicuous consumption*.[13] We attempt to outdo others who belong to the same social class as ourselves and attempt to gain the same level as the class above us by imitating them.[14] There are, in other words, two principles that are operative: *differentiation* inwards towards our own class, and *imitation* of the class above. Veblen claims that a player will not normally have the principle of conspicuous consumption as an explicit motive, and broadly speaking only be taken up with living as he or she feels is appropriate for a person of that particular social status.[15] It is no exaggeration to say that Veblen is critical of such a course of action. He feels, among other things, that it causes us to confuse economic and aesthetic worth,[16] and furthermore that fashionable apparel by nature is directly ugly, even though people are induced to believe that it is beautiful.[17] Veblen places simplicity and functionality as a norm, believing that everything that deviates from this is ugly and irrational, and therefore something that needs an explanation.

Like Veblen, Georg Simmel was no optimist regarding the future, but even so there is no doubt that he finds more of value in his own age that Veblen did. Simmel's theory is considerably more sophisticated than Veblen's. For him, it is not just a question of marking social status but of balancing opposing human needs and inclinations, such as individuality and conformity, freedom and independence.[18] Viewed thus, fashion becomes a unique phenomenon where 'all opposing main tendencies in the soul are represented'.[19] Simmel claimed that fashion cannot be found in societies where the socializing impulse is stronger than the differentiating, and where social classes have not formed. Such societies, which he referred to as 'primitive', are characterized by extremely stable styles.[20] If the styles last for too long they cannot be referred to as 'fashion', since fashions presuppose change. For Simmel, all fashions are by definition class fashions, and fashion is driven forwards by the upper classes discarding a fashion (and embracing a new one) as soon as the lower classes have imitated it.[21] He claimed that the more extensively a commodity is subject to the swift changes of fashion, the greater the need will become for cheap versions of it, because it will also be desired – unless in an inferior version – by the masses, who initially cannot afford the commodity.[22] It is precisely the production of these cheap versions that will promote the formation of a new fashion, because the item will no longer be as distinctive. So we arrive at the following circle: the faster fashion develops, the cheaper the items will become, and the cheaper the items become, the faster will fashion develop. In Simmel's essay 'Fashion' (1911), which is a revised and shortened edition of his *The Philosophy of Fashion*, Simmel claimed that fashion always carries its own death within it.[23] The aim of a fashion is always to be definitive for absolutely all individuals in a group, but if it attains that goal it will die, because it then neutralizes the actual opposition between conformity and individuality that is its basic definition. The classic explanation of the spread of fashion is then that it is created at the top of society and then trickles down the social strata. Another important work in this connection is *The Laws of Imitation* (1890) by the sociologist Gabriel de Tarde, for whom desire is made up of societal relations that follow certain 'laws of imitation'. It mainly functions by the lower classes imitating the upper ones, but Tarde emphasizes that modern society opens up a larger flexibility of imitation, so that the higher classes can also imitate the lower ones.[24] Here he is more perspicacious than Veblen and Simmel. By then such an imitation from the top downwards had already been taking place for some time.

One of the most telling examples of this development is what is perhaps the most revolutionary item of apparel in human history: the man's suit. Before the nineteenth century there was no essential difference between the apparel of upper-class men and women as regards ornamentation and the like: ornamentation was a question of class, not gender. What differences existed indicate that men were more sumptuously dressed than women. Industrialization and the economic and social changes that involves, however, created a need for simpler men's clothing for the new bourgeoisie. The brilliant solution to this need was the suit, which can be considered exemplary for the subsequent development of fashion. As Anne Hollander points out, male fashion took a radical leap into the modern era, while female fashion was left behind.[25] The suit signalled affiliation to a new age as well as distancing oneself from an aristocracy that was in the process of landing up in a historical backwater. With the suit we find a fashionable item of clothing that does the exact opposite of 'trickling down'. It was a middle-class garment that the upper class began to use. Urban fashions emerged that outdid aristocratic fashions and the like. There are even earlier examples of street fashion being adopted by higher social strata, as when the 'slashed' clothes worn by mercenary soldiers in the sixteenth century began to be adopted, admittedly in more refined versions, by higher classes – but this was an exception.

The suit has changed surprisingly little during the two centuries it has been in use. This is probably an important reason why male fashions have played such a modest role in the history of fashion.[26] Male fashion took such a quantum leap with the suit that it did not seem to develop very much subsequently, while female fashion constantly changed and, as such, was more interesting as the subject of research. In actual fact male fashion has also undergone a process of constant change, but these changes have been a good deal more subtle that in female fashion when it comes to cut, shades and fabrics. The use of tie, scarf and bows has varied a great deal. The cycles have, however, lasted longer than in female fashion, although since 1960 male fashion has also developed more rapidly, marked by such features as the emerging use of polo-necked sweaters, rather than a shirt and tie, and the adoption of a closer fit. In the 1970s male fashion began to become an attractive field for even the foremost couturiers, such as Yves Saint-Laurent. The suit established a norm, and much of the development of female fashion since then can be seen as gradually approaching it. It was not until the 1920s that female fashion began to 'catch up' with male fashion by getting closer to the simple style that had been the male norm for a century. Until the nineteenth century it was more usual for male fashion to adopt features of female fashion than the converse, but with the male suit the opposite applies. As Hollander points out, there was basically nothing 'modern' – understood here as an aesthetic norm that was very clearly realized in modernistic art and architecture – about female fashion before it began to imitate male fashion explicitly in the twentieth century.[27] It could perhaps be said that the objective was reached with Yves Saint-Laurent's woman's dinner jacket of 1965. Since then the distinction between male and female fashion has become less clear, in the sense that there has been a more fluid interaction between them. Even so, there are still certain items of clothing that are basically reserved for one gender. Despite repeated attempts, not least by Jean Paul Gaultier, to introduce the man's skirt, this is still a highly marginal item of clothing. The rhetoric that has surrounded male fashion has to a great extent been a set of denials: that there really does not exist anything we can call male fashions, that men do not dress on the basis of style (but only functionality), that men are not 'victims' of fashion in the same way as women.[28] But of course male fashion has a history, just as female fashion has, and the rules for men's apparel have been no less strict than those for women's. If anything, it could be claimed that male fashion has had stricter norms over the last two centuries because men have had fewer types of clothing to choose between.

We can find a similar development in trousers in general. Long trousers are known to have existed in antiquity, but it was not until the French Revolution that they became fashionable. The *sans culottes* ('those without knee-breeches') distanced themselves from the aristocracy and showed this by, among other things, rejecting their way of dressing. The *culotte* was an everyday garment for the aristocracy and the upper class in the eighteenth century. At first the term *sans culottes* was used pejoratively, but it later applied in a positive sense. Before the Revolution it was used ironically about those who could not afford silk stockings and knee-breeches (*culottes*) and so wore long trousers (*pantalons*) instead.[29] With the Revolution the fashion spread, and in England it was further developed and refined by, among others, the dandy Beau Brummell. Since this working-class garment had now reached the upper class, it was also made of silk.

This development is not completely unlike that from ordinary jeans to designer jeans.[30] Jeans started off by being a working-class garment and then moved up the social ladder. It is worth noting, however, that it did not go directly from the working to the middle class, but took a more complicated route.[31] After the workers, it was artists who wore jeans, then left-wing political activists and motorcycle gangs, something that gave jeans the nature of expressing an opposition to the status quo. This made them popular in youth cultures; since youthfulness had begun to become an aesthetic norm and the middle class wished to appear more youthful, it soon spread to the middle class. Once jeans had been accepted by the middle class they lost all their 'rebellious' force. Instead they became incorporated in a differentiation system. Initially, jeans were an 'egalitarian' item of clothing. Andy Warhol praised Coca-Cola for being an egalitarian product:

> A Coke is a Coke and no amount of money can get you a better Coke than the one the bum on the corner is drinking. All the Cokes are the same and all the Cokes are good. Liz Taylor knows it, the President knows it, the bum knows it, and you know it.[32]

He could have said the same about jeans, although the emergence of designer jeans – Yves Saint-Laurent was probably the first to include jeans in his collections in 1966 – changed all this: once jeans had an appeal apparent regardless of people's age and class, something had to be added to the item of clothing, partly by means of design and partly by attaching a brand label to the jeans. There is a large symbolic difference between jeans from Matalan and jeans from Versace. Thus, jeans became an example of dressing 'poor-man-style' in an explicitly expensive way. Chanel's 'little black dress' was an example of the same. Karl Lagerfeld has created clothes of shaved mink and mixed synthetic and genuine fur, which is a quite extreme variant of what Veblen referred to as 'conspicuous waste'.

The 'trickle-down' theory is only partially right, then, when we take a close look at the history of fashion. To a greater extent movement over the past forty years has been in the opposite direction, with perhaps its most striking expression in the 1990s with such styles as 'heroin chic', an extension of the Yves Saint-Laurent slogan 'Down with the Ritz – long live the street!' It is also a fact that those occupying a relatively safe position in the upper echelons of society have, generally speaking, been less concerned with following the latest fashions than those with a less well-established position in such strata. The new arrivals apparently had a greater need to be distinctive than those already established. From this point of view the 'trickle-down' factor did not apply from the very top – it is not here that the greatest innovators have been found. We can only confirm that considerable innovation has taken place in the lower classes as well, not least in the form of sometimes major modifications of upper-class fashions.

Innovation in other social strata has, however, been obscured by the fact that histories of fashion usually say a lot about what has been considered fashionable among the upper class in earlier periods, but we know considerably less about what sort of clothes were worn by the lower classes. There has been a tendency to focus on *haute couture* (high fashion), which is then considered the norm for fashions. In the past decades, however, it has become more and more usual to include the entire spectrum, from mass-produced fashion to *haute couture*.[33] And the relationship between the various parts of fashion is simply not one that starts at the top and then 'trickles down'. In the nineteenth century, there was a fairly limited spread to the lower social classes of what the upper class considered fashionable clothing.[34] The working class imitated clothing worn by higher classes to only a very limited extent, and when they did so the garments were often radically altered to make them more functional. On the whole, it would seem that functionality was more important than conforming to what the higher social classes might define as being fashionable. This does not mean, of course, that matters of taste were unimportant for the choice of clothing made in the lower ranks of society, but it was a different taste. Generally speaking, the working class has had what the sociologist Pierre Bourdieu describes as 'the taste of necessity', which is characterized by functionality.[35]

Why, then, did Veblen and, even more obviously, Simmel believe that the lower classes adopted the style of the upper class, even if somewhat belatedly? It is probably because the members of the working class that were actually *visible* had the sort of jobs where they were in contact with the middle and upper class and could be observed in the townscape.[36] We are dealing with such people as workmen, shop workers and servants – who dressed more 'finely' than most other workers – but only to a small extent with factory workers and the like. Like many others, Simmel generalized about the working class as a whole on the basis of the limited section with which he actually came in contact, but this generalization was partly misleading. What is right about Simmel's theory is that from the latter part of the nineteenth century onwards there were, to a certain extent, less visible differences between clothing worn by the various social classes than there had been before. Another important reason is that, as the century progressed, it became increasingly usual for uniforms and clothes linked to specific occupations to replace normal clothing, so that one's social status was clearly marked by the clothes one wore. This, without a doubt, can be seen as a strategy on the part of the upper class to make visible what 'position' the individual occupied, so that it was possible to counteract the incipient blurring of the differences between clothing in the various classes. Simmel's theory is not directly erroneous, but the picture was very much more complex than he assumed.

Even though Bourdieu has tried to distance himself from, among others, Veblen's theories, he follows the same model to a great extent. Bourdieu stresses that the driving force behind symbolic consumption is not primarily the imitation of the higher classes by the lower, rather the distinguishing strategies used by the higher classes with regard to the lower classes.[37] He describes how the acquisition of an aesthetic object, whether it be a painting or fashionable clothes, leads to the object being altered 'into a reified negation of all those not worthy to own it, through lacking the material or symbolic means required for acquiring it.'[38] For Bourdieu, taste is basically a negative category, a determination that works via negation and exclusion. He claims that so-called 'pure taste' has '*distaste* as its underlying principle'.[39] When taste is to be justified, this is done via the rejection of another taste. The determination of 'good' taste is achieved via the rejection of what is 'bad' taste. Bourdieu describes taste as a 'social sense of place'.[40] It is a sense that enables us to find our bearings in the social space, but it also assigns us a particular place in that space.

In this respect, Bourdieu broadly agrees with Veblen and Simmel, who consider fashion to be an upper-class invention, the aim of which is to create a distinction between themselves and the lower classes.[41] Bourdieu himself claims that his analyses of taste do not have anything to do with Veblen's theory because the latter's players deliberately sought distinctions, while for Bourdieu this basically occurs at a pre-conscious level.[42] But the difference is hardly as great as Bourdieu asserts. Veblen claims that a player will not normally have the principle of conspicuous consumption as his explicit motive,[43] but it has to be admitted that he often formulates himself in such a way that conspicuous consumption would precisely seem to be a conscious intention.[44] Despite everything, Bourdieu's diffusion model would basically seem to be the same as Veblen's: as the clothing of the upper class is gradually imitated by the lower class, it loses its exclusivity and has to be replaced by new fashions that can function as class markers. Therefore, the upper class becomes the driving force in the development of fashion, while the lower classes are passive copiers, taking over the fashions of the upper class in order to try and identify themselves with it. The middle class functions as a connecting link: as it strives upwards, it pulls with it the lower classes that it is trying to distinguish itself from.[45]

Bourdieu differs from Veblen in one important respect. For Veblen everything ultimately depends on economic capital. 'Symbolic' capital is only important as evidence of economic capital. Bourdieu reverses this and turns economic capital into a special instance of symbolic capital.[46] He has to do this, among other reasons, in order to be able to explain that there are artists who do not have economic capital and do not make any attempt to convert their cultural capital into economic capital – those who declare that they distance themselves from the entire economic field.[47] What can explain such behaviour if economic capital is ultimately the sole bringer of salvation? Bourdieu would either have to stand there without any explanation for this type of taste and aesthetic production, or have to open up a type of taste that calls for a separate explanation. This would be tantamount to opening up a kind of 'inherent taste', precisely what he has proposed to undermine. But, assuming that economic capital is merely an example of symbolic capital, he can incorporate practices that do not give any economic return, nor have any ambition to do so. In short, unlike Veblen's belief, 'good' taste in Bourdieu gives a return by being an expression of an affluence that is not only an indication of economic prosperity but is also more cultural by nature. As Bourdieu points out, all forms of capital are exposed to inflation. The distinctive value of objects is constantly declining as more and more gain possession of them. All capital is relationally determined in the sense that the value of anything depends on what others have. For anything to have a high value it is imperative that others do not have it. Something can have value simply because there is a scarcity. That is why it is important to make distinctions. It could be said that the point of the distinction is to *create* a scarcity, so that others are excluded, for only by excluding others can one gain possession of symbolic values.

There are social patterns of taste and these are embodied in what Bourdieu calls 'habitus'. This is 'a system of *personified schemata* which, formed in the course of collective history, have been acquired in the course of individual history, and which work *in a practical form and for a practical purpose*.'[48] Habitus mediates between the social field and the human body:

> A type of habitus (or a type of taste) corresponds to each class of positions, caused by the social conditioning that is linked to the corresponding conditions. And via the various forms of habitus and their ability to produce characteristics there corresponds a systematic unity of goods and characteristics that are linked to each other by a stylistic affinity.[49]

According to Bourdieu, habitus leads to 'systematic choices in the field of action (where the choices that are normally considered to be aesthetic make up one dimension)'.[50] This applies to such social divisions as class, gender, town and suburb, and low and high education. Taste is part of the construction social players implement of themselves and their surroundings. That is an important part of how a person with a particular taste is perceived by other arbiters of taste:

> Taste classifies, and taste classifies the person who classifies: subjects differ from each other in how they distinguish between the beautiful and the ugly, the exquisite and the common or vulgar, and via these distinctions the position the subjects themselves have within objective classifications is expressed or revealed.[51]

It is crucial to Bourdieu's analysis that *objective* social relations exist (i.e. social relations that are real), even though the players in the field of action have not themselves acknowledged their existence. It is a question of social structures that determine people's individual actions and preferences, but without these individuals having to become aware of these structures. What Bourdieu refers to as habitus enables us to believe that we have chosen what in actual fact is imposed on us. It appears to have been freely chosen, but in fact is a fairly direct reflection of an objective class affiliation. Presumptively autonomous taste is then, as Bourdieu sees it, anything but autonomous. Most of all he considers it to be a product and indicator of class affiliation:

> To the socially recognized hierarchy of art forms – and in turn within each of these, hierarchies of genres, schools and epochs – there corresponds a hierarchy of consumers. That is why taste is a particularly good marker of 'class'. Various ways of acquiring taste live on in ways of using what has been acquired.[52]

From this more sociological perspective, the idea of the autonomy of taste will be rather illusory. Here, taste is quite simply a function of class affiliation (or a wish for such). In philosophical aesthetics, taste is often asserted as an autonomous entity. This is perhaps particularly obvious in Kant, as long as the taste that is autonomous, or 'free', if you like, is considered as adequate. Bourdieu, on the other hand, claims that taste is by no means freely chosen. Admittedly we carry out aesthetic choices but, as Bourdieu sees it, the choice between Matalan and Prada is a *compulsory* choice. Economic considerations oblige the person with a poor economy to buy at Matalan – and the person concerned will presumably genuinely believe that Matalan has finer clothes than Prada. The person with a strong economy is similarly forced to choose Prada or some other 'exclusive' brand. However, it causes problems if taste is exclusively reduced to being a product of social fields. We experience taste as something highly personal. As La Rochefoucauld pointed out as far back as the mid-seventeenth century, our pride suffers more from having our taste rejected than our views. It is worse to hear that one has ugly clothes than that one has a confused view of national economic policy.

Bourdieu believes he has countered the objection that taste is something 'personal' by means of his habitus concept. The social conditioning is 'inscribed on the body', which in turn is a bearer of values:

> The difference can only become a sign – and a sign of *distinction*, of excellence (or vulgarity) – on the basis of a particular principle for viewing and dividing things. And this principle is a product of the personification of the structure of objective differences . . . and of those who attach value to the one or to others.[53]

Taste is not to be understood here as something 'inherent' but as something that is cultivated via social disciplining. It is a question of social structures that determine people's individual actions and preferences, but without these individuals necessarily having made themselves aware of these structures. Normally, they will *not* be aware of them.

In many respects Bourdieu operates within a perspective where taste has to be explained on the basis of the class-differentiating principle, and where fashion is propelled by this differentiation. A fundamental problem about these analyses, however, is that they are strongly based on a class concept that basically no longer operates. The problem is not least that Bourdieu presupposes a kind of uniform, distinct and objective space, where cultural capital functions as a kind of universally accepted medium of exchange. But such an objective space hardly exists. Bourdieu admits that cultural distinctions are expressed in different ways in different fields, but he believes even so that there is a kind of objective organizational principle that can explain these differences. 'Class' becomes a main category that can absorb all other differences such as age, gender, race and ethnicity. It is doubtful whether the class concept is able to bear such a burden. Not least, it becomes awkward to deal with such small, local, inward distinctions as subcultures from such a perspective, since taste in the higher classes will often be irrelevant in order to understand them. We are dealing here with taste as an important *internal* factor of the individual subculture.

The emergence of modern individualism, where taste to an increasing extent becomes an individual concern and the class concepts have to a great extent outplayed their role, leads to Bourdieu's perspective losing much of its explanatory force. When taste no longer makes me a member of a social group but, on the contrary, serves to show who I am as a completely unique individual, other theories than that of Bourdieu will presumably have to be used. There will, of course, continue to be differences of taste, but these will be more individual than those that are class-orientated. To the extent that they are enacted in groups, these groups can scarcely be ordered into a more general social space. Instead, we find a plurality of partially overlapping groupings that have no hierarchical order. And in this plurality there is no one group that can install its taste as the most legitimate, as the actual 'taste standard'. In short, we get a social space where distinctions can be made, and these distinctions can most definitely result in cultural and social capital – but this capital cannot be incorporated into any objective social hierarchy.

One problem present in all models to explain fashion on the basis of class differentiation, by which changes are driven forwards by the higher social classes because fashion has been diluted by imitations in the lower classes, is that the horizontal flow of 'new' objects that replace the 'old' ones often moves faster than the vertical spread to other social strata. The replacement at the horizontal level, then, develops relatively independently in relation to the vertical imitation. Furthermore, we have already pointed out that the vertical imitation is not just a 'trickling down'. It is perhaps possible to claim that it anticipates imitation and attempts to preclude it by already having put behind it what is expected to be imitated. But this looks like an *ad hoc* argument. Bourdieu emphasizes that it would be naïve 'not to notice that fashions, when it comes to clothing and make-up, are a completely essential element in a form of mastery'.[54] It is also possible to raise the objection against Bourdieu that, even though the struggle for such as social position is undoubtedly part of the field of fashion, it is misleading to claim that this could explain the origin of fashion. It arose first among a social elite that did not need to concern itself unduly about its social status precisely by virtue of its prominent position.

The sociologist Herbert Blumer was one of the first critics of the theory that the development of fashion ought to be explained on the basis of class differentiation:

> The efforts of an elite class to set itself apart in appearance takes place inside of the movement of fashion instead of being its cause. The prestige of elite groups, in place of setting the direction of the fashion movement, is effective only to the extent to which they are recognized as representing and portraying the movement. The people in other classes who consciously follow the fashion do so because it is the fashion and not because of the separate prestige of the elite group. The fashion dies not because it has been discarded by the elite group but because it gives way to a new model more consonant with developing taste. The fashion mechanism appears not in response to a need of class differentiation and class emulation but in response to a wish to be in fashion, to be abreast of what has good standing, to express new tastes which are emerging in a changing world.[55]

For Blumer, then, the explanation lies not in class differentiation but in a kind of collective and changing taste that the fashion-conscious wish to keep abreast of, or preferably anticipate. While Veblen, Simmel and Bourdieu place class differentiation before the fashion process and feel that it is simply reproduced in fashion, Blumer's perspective implies that an elite is constituted by the actual fashion process itself: fashion develops according to its own logic, and the 'elite' consists of those who manage to exploit this development faster than others, and thereby create their own status by keeping abreast of their time. The idea of collective selection has the advantage of opening up a balanced view of the diffusion of fashion. As I have pointed out, fashion – especially over the past forty to fifty years – has *not* followed a diffusion model downwards from above. The problem with Blumer's theory is that it is so vague as to be practically devoid of any explanatory force.[56]

Blumer's theory comes close to referring to a kind of spirit of the age (*Zeitgeist*), and there are a number of theorists who explicitly ascribe to the most successful trendsetters a special ability to grasp such a spirit – and actually to anticipate it.[57] Even the historian Eric Hobsbawm wrote: 'How brilliant trendsetters, a notoriously hard group to analyse, sometimes succeed better in predicting the shapes of the future than professional forecasters is one of the most obscure questions of history – and for the cultural historian one of the most central.'[58] The problem is that it is notoriously difficult to define accurately the 'spirit of the age', especially when fashions change as quickly as they have over the last few decades, and when a fashion cycle may be so brief that it hardly lasts a season. The reference to a spirit of the age would have sounded more plausible if fashion cycles lasted as long as they used to do. One could possibly claim that today's 'spirit of the age' is an unrestricted pluralism with extremely fast changes, and that this is reflected in present-day fashion. The problem is that this would not explain why, despite everything, there is often a certain coincidence in style between various designers during a given season. Fashions ought rather then to spread out in all directions. Moreover, while one would certainly believe that the most central events of recent times – such as the fall of the Berlin Wall, the genocide in Bosnia or the fight against terror after 11 September 2001 – were an important part of the 'spirit of the age', it is difficult to claim that they have made any noticeable impact on the fashion scene, even though there have been odd references to military uniforms and the like. In short, the reference to a spirit of the age functions badly as an explanation of the development of fashion.

A really trivial explanation of why fashions change as they do would be that the fashion houses, to a great extent, are simply following the advice of the so-called 'fashion forecasters' in Paris and London regarding what they think will be 'in' in a year or two, and thus help to ensure that such prophecies become self-fulfilling.[59] When such advice coincides, we see a coincidence in the fashions launched by the fashion houses, and when the advice diverges, there is a corresponding spread in the fashions. What 'scientific' basis these fashion forecasters have for their prophecies is, of course, quite a different matter. As long as they can supply self-fulfilling prophecies, they have defended their right to exist towards the fashion industry.

It is possible today to distinguish between three main categories in fashion: luxury fashion, industrial fashion and street fashion.[60] Luxury fashion is to be found at the high end of the price range and is made to measure – the most expensive section being *haute couture*. Industrial fashion is mass-produced, but ranges from expensive designer clothes to the inexpensive clothes chains. Street fashion is created from various subcultures. There are also seamless transitions between the three categories. What starts as a subculture is often brought into limited production within the same subculture, but it can then spread into industrial fashion, and later be adopted by luxury fashion – or vice versa. As *haute couture* is increasingly leaving the market – today there are only about 2,000 customers worldwide and about 4,500 employees – some off-the-peg clothing (*prêt-à-porter*) has acquired a status (and a price tag) that was previously reserved for *haute couture*. Many of today's most high-profile couturiers operate exclusively with *prêt-à-porter* and have dropped *haute couture*. While mass-produced clothing had formerly mainly been watered-down, belated versions of 'real' fashion (*haute couture*), from the 1960s *prêt-à-porter* began to make its mark as 'adequate' fashion, despite the fact that it is mass-produced. Instead of representing the spearhead of fashion trends, *haute couture* began to lag behind. When trousers were finally included in *haute couture* collections for women, they were already so widespread that more trousers were being produced for women than skirts in industrial fashion. Of course, much *haute couture* has also been created with the intention of being at the leading edge of fashion. The avant-garde fashion created within large sections of *haute couture* became increasingly spectacular, but at the same time it had a decreasing influence on the rest of the field of fashion. Collections from couturiers such as Jean Paul Gaultier and Rei Kawakubo have challenged widespread conceptions of beauty ideals, but this has only spread to a small extent to clothing that is actually worn. And when these couturiers make mass fashion – such as Kawakubo's shirts for Fred Perry in 2004 – the items are normally extremely conventional. Glamour has now allegedly returned to *haute couture* after devoting itself to the opposite for a decade in the 1990s, although there are no strong signs of this in mass fashion. *Haute couture* is simply no longer in a position to prescribe what is 'in' and what is 'out'.

Formerly there was a much greater consensus among designers and a more centralized model, unlike today's more decentralized and differentiated fashion production. There were far fewer 'important' couturiers, and these were more in agreement when it came to such matters as cut, shades and length of skirts for the season in question. Naturally, competition among couturiers about setting a standard ensured that there were also variations, but their collections were much more similar than is the case in more recent *haute couture*. It could be said that there was a centre (Paris) that defined one norm and that only those who wore clothes that conformed to this norm were 'fashionable'. This consensus has more or less disappeared over recent decades and the notion that there is only one norm for fashion has broken down. Instead, there are a number of smaller fashion centres and norms. It is precisely this dispersal that has prompted a demand for agencies prepared to predict how trends will develop. The advice they provide for fashion houses can help to explain why fashions often conform to the same trend during a season, even though designers are more widely spread than before.

The challenge for consumers is not in having clothes that are 'fashionable' but rather in deciding which fashion one intends to follow. It is not true that 'everything is allowed'. What has happened is rather that there is a plurality of norms that exist side by side. Taken separately, these norms can be just as rigorous as before – even though clothes norms tend to have become a bit looser – but the individual, to a greater extent than previously, may now hop from norm to norm and sometimes wear clothes that cross over various norms. Certain contexts, however, still demand tight restrictions. One does not come to an audience with the monarch dressed in a T-shirt and jeans with holes in them, while in the workplace there are often relatively strict clothes regulations. More people used to wear some form of uniform when at work, whether a boiler suit or protective clothing 'on the workshop floor', or a suit and tie (or formal attire) at the office ('blue collar' and 'white collar' workers). As the focus increased on 'creativity' and 'individuality' – two words that would seem to be the mantras of our age – these norms have apparently become much looser. In the 1990s, for example, 'Dress Down Friday' became popular, with the suit left in the wardrobe back home and people turning up to work in 'leisurewear'. The interesting thing, however, was that the norm for this presumptively relaxed garb was just as strict as the clothes regulations on the other days. Everyone was 'off work' in the same way, with the same type of trousers, shirt and jacket. It would not have been tolerated to turn up in body-hugging latex, or a washed-out sweatsuit, even though these were actually the clothes normally worn at weekends. All that was done was to replace one code of clothing by another that was little freer than that imposed on other working days.

Gilles Lipovetsky writes: 'After the monopolistic and aristocratic system of *haute couture*, fashion has arrived at a democratic pluralism of labels'.[61] It is not unreasonable to claim that fashion has become more democratic – but it has not become egalitarian. Even though it is not possible to order the brands in a strict hierarchy, and the symbolic value of the brands varies from year to year, certain brands undeniably enjoy a higher standing than others in the fashion system. Paul Smith, for example, is more prestigious than Batistini when it comes to men's suits. Nor is it all that simple to see what occupational group or social class a given person belongs to. If we turn the clocks back a century, it was normally easy to distinguish different occupational groups in the street. It was obvious who were manual workers, servants, office workers and the like, and it was even more obvious who belonged to the upper class. This is a hard task today, even though it is quite obvious that a person with a tool-belt is probably a workman and one wearing a suit from Paul Smith is hardly a job-seeker.

Today, however, diffusion patterns follow age rather than income and assets, in that fashion begins with younger consumers and then spreads to those who are older. It could be said that this trend started as far back as the Romantic period, when the emphasis on the 'natural' led to a movement towards simpler apparel that had previously been the sole preserve of children (and the lower social classes). Ever younger children wear 'adult' fashions, and adults are increasingly wearing 'youth' fashions. Since the 1980s, in particular, it has become difficult to distinguish various age groups from each other. If we live in an instantaneous culture, it is hardly surprising that our ideals are drawn from something that to an eminent degree is underway and unfinished: youth. At the same time, 'youth' is stretched out further and further, so that increasingly it becomes a permanent state rather than being a transitional phase. 'Youth' is in the process of ceasing to be a term for a particular age group and tending to be a term for an 'attitude' towards life.

Diffusion does not have any distinct principle and spreads more inwards between various segments rather than 'trickling down' from one segment to another. If we look at fashions in the lower price brackets, we now find items of clothing that have been more or less independently designed and are not inferior copies of more expensive fashions.[62] The mass market has also become individualized. Mass-produced articles are, to an increasing extent, launched in many different variants, with different accessories that offer a large combination potential so the single consumer can create his or her 'individual' expression. This neutralizes the opposition between mass production and individuality. Hereafter, fashion is more a question of individual choice, not so much one of following instructions from a particular centre. On the other hand it is possible to ask just how individual these choices actually are, when the major chains account for three-quarters of turnover on clothes, buying in and producing clothes on the basis of advice from the same fashion forecasters.

It is probably fairly futile to attempt to find an 'algorithm' for changes in fashion, with regard to both clothing and other phenomena, even though quite a few such attempts have been made. Lipovetsky states that change in fashion cannot be derived from a single diffusion principle. It is more probable that novelty has an attractive force in itself and does not need to be explained on the basis of a social distinction mechanism.[63] As we saw in chapter Two, there are grounds, however, for doubting whether fashion is able any longer to provide us with anything 'new'. Does it then have any other characteristics? Can it, for example, function as a means of communication?

4

Fashion and Language

> For the first time she thought seriously about clothes. Apart from warmth, protection and propriety, what was the idea of clothes exactly? . . . Patently the idea was to express something through the medium of shape and colour. But express what? Were clothes just saying 'Look!'? Money and sex seemed to be the main commodities on offer here. Clothes could deny or affirm either of these. Mary speculated what her own clothes might have to say on the topics of money and sex. Could clothes express a lack of one and a simple bafflement about the other? Yes, but that wasn't what clothes were in business to do; that wasn't clothes' line; that wasn't what clothes were keen on expressing. Clothes were interested in other things, in abundance and expertise. Obliquely and perhaps inadvertently, clothes also did a third thing: they told other people about the soul they encased by dramatizing your attempted lies about money and sex . . .
>
> Martin Amis[1]

Symbols are central to all shaping of identity, whether it be a crucifix, a safety pin that pierces the skin or a national costume. These symbols have to *mean* something and help say something about the person wearing the symbol. Certain colours, for example, are associated with political sympathies, such as anarchism and the combination of red and black. In earlier societies – feudal societies not least – dress codes were relatively stable, being able to convey the social identity of the wearer fairly unambiguously. Much of this stability, however, disappeared with the advent of modernity, so clothing has become a less clear indication of a person's identity.[2] During the eighteenth century it became increasingly less usual to give items of clothing decorative motifs with a specific significance, the emphasis instead being more on cut and texture. This resulted in clothes that were less able to give a clear indication of the wearer's identity. Even so, we still draw conclusions about people on the basis of their clothes. If we see someone in full S&M gear, we assume that the person has sexual preferences that lie in this area. And if we see a man looking as if he has stepped out of a print by Tom of Finland (Touko Laaksonen), we will assume that he is gay. If we see a political leader in military uniform, we assume that that person leads a highly militarized group or state. These are clothes with clear symbolic values, but the picture is made more complicated by the fact that mass fashion has absorbed elements of military, fetish and gay clothing, and that these clothes are also worn by people whose identity in no way matches the origins of the garments. And even though certain types of clothes communicate quite clearly, at least to specific groups that can read the codes, it is not a given that *all* clothes communicate in this way.

Perhaps the most extreme (and least convincing) attempt to consider clothes as language is to be found in *The Language of Clothes* by Alison Lurie. As the author points out at the beginning of her book, clothes must make up a vocabulary and have a grammar if they are going to constitute a language.[3] She claims that in principle this vocabulary is at least as large as every spoken language, 'since it includes every article of clothing, hairstyle and body decoration that has ever been invented.' In addition, clothing comprises a number of dialects, accents, archaisms, loan words and slang. In other words, the analogy with language is taken very far indeed. According to Lurie, there is a proportional relation between the number of items of clothing one has and how much one is able to express visually, because clothes are one's visual vocabulary.[4] So a person with a small wardrobe can express only a few messages via clothes, while someone interested in fashion with a large wardrobe is able to express a number of different messages. But there is no reason to believe that this is so. Most clothes communicate so little that even a large wardrobe will not communicate all that much, so it is doubtful that the average slave of fashion should be ascribed any greater visual ability to communicate than, for example, a person who only has a few items of clothing but who indicates a distinct subcultural affiliation.

Lurie also claims to have found a number of equivalents to 'psychological speech defects' in clothing:

> We will hear, or rather see, the repetitive manner of a man who always wears the same jacket or a pair of shoes whatever the climate or occasion; the childish lisp of the woman who clings to the frills and ribbons of her early youth; and those embarrassing lapses of the tongue – or rather of the garment – of which the classical examples are the unzipped fly and the slip that becomes a social error. We will also notice the signs of more temporary inner distress: the too-loud or harsh 'voice' that exhausts our eye rather than our ear with glaring colors and clashing patterns, and the drab colorless equivalent of the inability to speak above a whisper.[5]

These analogies are not particularly convincing, and the highly direct manner in which Lurie interprets everything often comes close to unintentional parody, as when she claims that a tie in bright colours expresses virility, or that a clergyman without a tie has been 'symbolically castrated'.[6]

Lurie's entire book is based on a loose analogy between clothing and language, but the analogy professes to be more than this, claiming that clothing *is* language.[7] No attempt is made anywhere in the book to justify the assertion that clothing really can be considered as language. It simply remains a loose assertion that is only supported by a series of analogies, many of which are extremely dubious. She has in no way supplied a *theory* as to how we could consider clothes as a language. Obviously clothes communicate something, but what is it? They cannot be said as a matter of course to express a *message*. The sociologist Fred Davis introduces a comic strip from *The New Yorker*, in which the character Rhonda Perlmutter III has a hat that says 'My favorite food is tuna', a handbag that says 'Someday I'd like to see a UFO' and a skirt that says 'My mother lives in Sacramento, but we speak quite often on the telephone'.[8] Obviously, clothes do *not* communicate in such a way.

Roland Barthes has made what is perhaps the most theoretically ambitious attempt to consider clothes as a kind of language. His book on the fashion system was first published in 1967, but it was begun a decade earlier. Even at the time of publication Barthes considered it in some way a failure. It is fairly unreadable and seems quite a bit longer than the 350 pages of its English edition. Barthes sets himself the task of studying 'the fashion system', which he defines as the totality of the social relations and activities that are necessary for fashion to exist. He distinguishes initially between three aspects of clothing: the real garment, the represented garment and the used garment. These are three forms of existence applied to the garment on its path through the fashion system. The 'real' garment is the actual physical garment that is produced, the 'represented' garment is that which is displayed in fashion magazines and advertising, and the 'used' garment is what is bought and worn. In his book Barthes is mainly interested in the 'represented' garment, because that is what we are presented with as consumers. What we meet is a garment that has always already been represented, and which has always been definitively shaped by a fashion discourse. Barthes therefore insists that it is impossible to place the 'real' garment ahead of the fashion discourse, and that the order ought instead to be reversed so that it moves from a constituting discourse (the 'represented' garment) to the reality that is constituted.[9] To be 'fashionable' has nothing to do with the material characteristics of clothes, in Barthes' opinion, but is a product of the fashion language. To understand fashion, it is therefore necessary to try to understand the language that constitutes it *as* fashion. Barthes states his wish to study 'written garments', clothes without any practical function, as described in fashion magazines, because only the 'meaning' is left when the function is removed.[10] Furthermore, Barthes claims, the 'written garment' does not contain any 'vague temporality'. This is important because he wishes to carry out a synchronic study of fashion rather than a diachronic one. In other words, he wants to study a static fashion system. This is an original move, since most studies of fashion are diachronic and deal with the historical transformation of clothing, but it can be objected that adopting a perspective in which fashion is 'frozen' in an instant removes precisely the temporality that is the essence of fashion.

In accordance with the structuralist theory of Ferdinand de Saussure, Barthes strictly distinguishes between the signifier (*signifiant*) and the signified (*signifié*), which may be interpreted as a division between the material side of a sign and its content side, such as the sound-image of the word 'trousers' and the meaning of the word. Each sign must contain both these aspects of content and expression, but the link between the two is *arbitrary*. There is no necessary link between sound-image and meaning for the sign 'trousers'. Other languages have quite different signifiers for the same object signified. This is an important point to remember when studying fashion. The relation between a garment and a meaning is completely arbitrary. The reason why so many people talk in a misleading way about 'clothes as language' is that they seem to believe that a given form or colour of a garment has a non-arbitrary relation to a given meaning. Despite the arbitrary relation between signifier and signified, there is a regulated relation between them via a 'code', a set of shared rules that link the signifier with the signified. If one is unfamiliar with the code, it is impossible to orientate oneself in the system. One will be unable to understand that a suit and tie have a more 'formal' meaning than a suit without a tie, since the tie in itself – as a 'real' item of clothing (i.e. as a material object) – does not indicate formality. Barthes emphasizes that there is a very complex relationship between the signifier and the signified in clothing. Even though an open-necked shirt is meant to signify a relaxed attitude, and even though we can say that it is the opening that indicates this relaxation, it is not given that every opening, in a skirt for example, will indicate a relaxed attitude.[11]

Nothing very much emerges from Barthes' analysis of the fashion system. He describes the rhetoric of clothing as 'impoverished', that it expresses only highly banal meanings.[12] It never offers any deeper meaning and is in fact devoid of content.[13] There can hardly be many people who would assess Barthes' attempt at a 'scientific' study of fashion as being particularly successful. It is, on the other hand, more successful in a political respect, and ultimately what Barthes is attempting to carry out in his book is a political project. Fashion 'mythologizes'. Mythologization is understood by Barthes as a process by which the contingent and historical are raised to something necessary and universally valid, and Barthes is engaged in a de-mythologization project aimed at unveiling the myth *as* a myth, so that we can become emancipated from it. He claims that fashion is tyrannical and that its signs are arbitrary, and for precisely that reason it has to reform the sign into a 'natural fact'.[14] There is no 'natural' reason for a dinner jacket being considered 'neater' than jeans and a T-shirt, or for one set of clothes being appropriate to wear at a wedding and the other one not. There is no 'natural' reason for trousers being considered a specifically 'masculine' item of clothing across long stretches of the history of fashion. The tenuous 'meaning' garments have is completely arbitrary, so there is little reason to be bound by such meaning.

What does a garment 'mean'? Where does it get its meaning from? It could be tempting to say that a garment means what the designer intended it to mean. This line of approach, however, is problematic. In contemporary hermeneutics there is broad agreement that an artist does not stand in a privileged position when it comes to understanding the works he or she creates. The artist is quite simply an interpreter on an equal footing with all other interpreters.[15] This line of approach would also have difficulties in accounting for the fact that clothes change meaning from context to context, and they ought not to do so if the designer's intention determined their meaning.

The next alternative could be that the meaning can be found in the consciousness of the person wearing the garment. A garment would then mean this or that according to what the wearer of the garment thinks it means. But that is not particularly plausible, either. I cannot simply put on a black suit and claim that this suit says: 'I am worried about the consequences of globalization's impact on the cultural diversity of the world.' Nor can I put on a ragged pair of jeans and a faded T-shirt and claim that I am formally dressed. This is quite simply not a formal kind of attire, no matter what intentions I might claim to have by wearing it. Moreover, clothes can have meanings of which the wearer is unaware. Someone unfamiliar with the colour codes current in gang environments in major US cities, for example, and who moves into the wrong area with the wrong colour T-shirt, could end up in a great deal of trouble. Even though that person does not intend anything by wearing that colour, others might ascribe a particular meaning to a T-shirt with such a colour in a particular environment.

Is it then onlookers who decide the meaning of a garment? It is not that simple, either. Suppose that a person is wearing clothing with Germanic symbols on it and this is interpreted by some onlookers as meaning that the person has political leanings far out to the right, as these symbols are also used in such environments. Does this mean that the wearer is expressing Nazi values? If the person explains to the onlookers that he or she is actually an anti-Nazi but also a believer in the Germanic gods, they would – if reasonable people – revise their interpretation. So the interpretation of onlookers cannot be set to determine the meaning of clothing, either.

There would appear to be only one alternative left: the meaning must lie in the garment itself. But not even this is particularly convincing, since firstly it is difficult to understand how a black suit or a pair of red trousers could have a meaning 'in itself'. If all context is removed from a garment, all meaning is also removed. Furthermore, this line of approach would find it difficult to explain how a garment can change meaning so drastically according to time and place. To all appearances it would seem to be misplaced to look for one source that can determine the meaning of a garment, since to a greater extent it arises and exists in the spaces between people and between people and the world – where different interpretations clash, where no instance can elevate itself to an absolute authority that defines the meaning of the garment, and where no final meaning can ever be fixed.

Strictly speaking, clothes are *not* a language. It is often claimed that they are, but they have neither grammar nor vocabulary in any usual sense. Whereas it is clear that they communicate something, not everything that communicates ought to be called a language. Clothes can be considered semantically coded, but it is a code with a highly tenuous and unstable semantics, without any really hard-and-fast rules. Words too change their meaning according to time and place, but verbal language is quite stable compared to the semantic changes of clothing. It is not least for that reason that the structuralist approach to clothes fashions does not work very well, because this method presupposes fairly stable meanings. It is no coincidence that it was his work on *The Fashion System* book that led Roland Barthes to abandon classic structuralism. Rather than being a language in any normal sense, it can be tempting to describe fashionwear as a 'visual tongue', to borrow an expression from the writer Hermann Broch.[16] In that sense, clothes are closer to music and visual art than to normal language.

Clothes are semantically unstable because the meaning is directly related to context. The sociologist Diana Crane claims that, when clothes are considered as *texts*, it was typical in hierarchical societies for clothes to function as 'closed' texts with a relatively stable, fixed meaning. In more fragmentary postmodern societies, on the other hand, clothes function more as 'open' texts that can constantly acquire new meanings.[17] This is not least due to different groups wanting to use the same items of clothing but to ascribe considerably different meaning to them. The time aspect also plays a role. In every society there are clothes that communicate something about the wearer, and this presupposes some shared concept of what particular clothes are to signify. These conceptions, however, are subject to constant change. Anne Hollander has demonstrated how even black clothes, which are presumably the most semantically stable clothes to have been made, have radically changed their meaning over time.[18]

Apart from semantic instability, another great problem encountered by clothes fashions as suppliers of meaning is that they have a tendency to lose meaning quickly as the fashion spreads. A word does not lose its meaning in the same sense when it becomes more widespread. When garments that have a certain meaning potential (such garments will often be subcultural) are introduced into other contexts, for example on the cat-walk, and then out to a wider public, they lose meaning: the more widespread, the less meaningful. Therefore fashion is also a constant battle to fill out meaning that is being worn away at increasing speed. These meanings are often filled out via references to the world beyond fashion – often in quite banal ways, as when we suddenly saw a number of military effects on the cat-walks in autumn 2001. First and foremost, however, fashions are created from earlier fashions that can be recirculated and combined *ad infinitum*. Like art, fashion has become ever more self-referential. It is created by previous fashions that can be affirmed or made fun of. This also involves a recirculation of earlier meanings, which are now combined in all sorts of ways, with the result that the cultural and political meanings the garments might once have had disappear in an ever weaker cacophony.

That is why a good deal of fashion is characterized by a desperate attempt to say something. If one is to sell symbolic values, these symbols must be made to represent something. They must be filled out with some content or other. An important part of this process takes place via *haute couture*, which is no longer mainly a matter of clothing but of images: it is an investment in a brand name, so that *prêt-à-porter* collections, licence products and other goods can be sold. It is extremely doubtful if John Galliano's creation *Sylvia* for Christian Dior Haute Couture (autumn–winter 2000 collection), in which the model looks like a cross between a human being and a horse, will ever be worn by anyone else than the model at the fashion show. These are not clothes to be *used* – their utility value is completely irrelevant. There is a consideration that is above all others: maximum pre-exposure. It has been estimated that a 20-minute fashion show that costs $500,000 to produce generates advertising to the tune of $7 million in the US alone – and considerably more in the world as a whole.[19] That is obviously the reason why so many of the major fashion houses have employed presumptively controversial designers who could give fashion a 'content'. In recent years we have seen a return to extravagance and deliberate flaunting of luxury that would seem to have a limited need to *say* anything. This can be seen as an admission that today's fashion is more or less incapable of communicating anything of meaning.

It is possible to argue that subcultural clothes have a more definable 'meaning' than mass fashion. That is true to some degree, but the subcultures are also undergoing change. The sociologist David Muggleton claims that subcultures have been replaced by 'post-subcultures', whose members are less preoccupied about maintaining ideological and stylistic distinctions from other groups, and that the members of these groups typically go in for 'style surfing' – a move between various styles – rather than sticking to just one style.[20] It is problematic talking about subcultures at all when there no longer exists a uniform, dominant culture that subcultures can define themselves against. Mass culture itself has become so fragmentary and pluralistic that the boundaries between subculture and mass culture have become very indistinct. This is clearly why subcultures are becoming less reliable suppliers of 'meaningful' clothes.

A style of dress in the feudal period, for example, was able to communicate a 'message', but the same hardly applies to postmodern fashion. It does not communicate a message – it *is* the actual message. It is not so much a question of a semantic code as an aesthetic effect. To the extent it says anything, it is something in the nature of 'Look at me!' In more closed subcultures it is obvious that clothing can have a more distinct and unambiguous meaning, but this can hardly be transferred to mass fashion. We cannot exclude the possibility that fashion can 'say something', but as a means of communication clothes are generally speaking rather unsuitable. If one has a 'message' to the outside world, it would probably be considerably more effective to say it with words than don presumptively meaning-conveying apparel.

5

Fashion and the Body

Arms are the new breasts.
Bret Easton Ellis[1]

I believe in plastic surgery.
Andy Warhol[2]

Skin is in.
Absolutely Fabulous[3]

The shaping of self-identity in the postmodern era is in a crucial sense a *body project*. We can see the body to an increasing extent tending to become seminal for an understanding of self-identity.[4] The ego is very much constituted via the presentation of the *body*. We can also see this in relation to a number of practices, such as asceticism or a diet, which formerly had a more spiritual purpose, but now mainly have to do with shaping the body. Only in the late Victorian period did people begin to go on diets in order to achieve a specifically *aesthetic* ideal.[5] Admittedly the aristocracy in Hellenic culture maintained an ideal of moderation in food intake because this indicated self-control. Similarly fasting was a central Christian practice in the Middle Ages, indicating that the spirit was stronger than the flesh. But the crucial difference was that these practices had less to do with the body in isolation than with the spirit housed in this body. In addition, these were practices found mainly in the highest echelons of society. Late

 Victorian dieting, on the other hand, was a phenomenon that spread to the middle class and had to do with regulating food intake in such a way that an idealized, slim *body* was to be the result. The 'spiritual' aspects of the diet were distinctly subordinate. This does not mean that all 'spiritual' connotations were absent. Obesity was, and to a great extent still is, considered to be an indicator of such moral and mental qualities as laziness and lack of will-power. The vital thing is that it was not out of respect for these mental qualities that the dieting was undertaken: it was motivated by a desire to shape the body, not the soul. This trend has only accelerated since then.

In the case of a traditional dualism between the soul and the body, as especially found in Platonic and Christian traditions, the identity of the body will be relatively unimportant, because identity will primarily have to do with the soul, not the body. Increasingly, however, it is the body that has taken centre stage in connection with the shaping of identity. Jean Baudrillard writes that the body has taken over the soul's moral and ideological role as an object of salvation.[6] So Oscar Wilde has a point when he points out: 'To be really mediæval one should have no body. To be really modern one should have no soul.'[7] The body has become an especially privileged fashion object. It appears to be something plastic that can constantly change to fit new norms as they emerge. It is tempting to say that the body has changed places with consciousness – as understood in empiricism – as a *tabula rasa*, a clean slate, on which anything can be inscribed.[8]

Hegel emphasizes that body and clothing are distinct, and they must both be allowed to develop freely.[9] Here he might seem to be anticipating Simmel's later point that clothes become objectivized, in the sense that they become detached from their starting point in the needs of the subject – in this case the need of the body for clothing. But while Simmel sees this as a 'tragedy of culture', because the opposition between subject and object is integrated into the subject, which then becomes objectivized, Hegel feels it is completely legitimate. Hegel also writes that dependence on fashion is preferable to dependence on nature.[10] The fashion designer Elsa Schiaparelli claimed that clothes ought not to be adapted to the body, but the body ought rather to be adapted to clothes.[11] We squeeze our feet, for example, into shoes that are heteromorphous in relation to our feet. Inspired by Magritte's painting *Red Model* (1935), a number of designers, including Pierre Cardin (1986) and Vivienne Westwood (2000), have also made shoes that are shaped like feet, to accentuate the usual difference of form between feet and shoes. Ever since it began, fashion has displayed relative freedom in relation to body shape, but the body and clothes have always been in a 'dialogue' with each other, with the shape of the body influencing fashion and vice versa.

We seek identity in the body, and clothes are an immediate continuation of the body.[12] That is also why clothes are so important to us: they are closest to our body. Our perception of the human body is influenced to an amazing extent by the fashions prevalent at the time. Anne Hollander has shed light on this in her book *Seeing through Clothes*, in which she demonstrates how portraits of nudes continually show the models as if they were dressed, even though it is patently obvious they are not.[13] In periods where corsets were extensively used, we can see the absent corset shaping the naked body more than can be explained by the fact that the corsets had influenced body shape in a purely physiological manner. Stays and bustles in dresses gave rise to naked figures with thin waists and broad hips. When dresses were contracted just below the breasts and allowed to billow out further down, the nudes acquired quite sturdy bellies. Clothes rewrite the body, give it a different shape and a different expression. This applies not only to the clothed body but also to the unclothed; or, more precisely, the unclothed body is always also clothed. Our perception of the human body is always dependent on the prevailing fashions of the time, and our perception of fashions is in turn dependent on their visual representation in paintings, photographs and other media. For many centuries this particularly applied to the few who could afford to buy works of art or be invited to places where they were to be found. In the nineteenth and twentieth centuries, however, pictures became accessible to all because of the new reproductive techniques. Human perception never depicts neutrally, it interprets, and the interpretations depend on people's perceptual habits: what we *see* when we look at something depends on what we have seen previously. The visual dressing of the naked body with invisible clothes that shape it does not only apply to artistic representations but also to live experience.[14]

In the final scene of Robert Altman's film *Prêt-à-Porter* (1994), a pregnant woman played by Ute Lemper, naked except for a bridal veil, moves along the cat-walk. The audience at the fashion show are sceptical at first, but then applaud this as a creative fashion move. Altman possibly wants to say something here about the emperor's new clothes, or the like, but I would more like to claim that the scene does not say all that much. Nakedness only says something by being in a dialogue with clothes. At the same time, naked skin has clearly become increasingly central in fashion. If we look back at the fashion photographs of the 1950s, they normally showed women in their twenties in middle-class environments, but the *clothes* were the centre of interest. In the 1960s there was a distinctly stronger emphasis on youthfulness – and, not least, a great deal more skin was being shown. Since then this development has only intensified, with a constant feature being that the clothes themselves have faded further into the background in fashion photography. Rather than present clothes, it has been a matter of presenting an *image* in which the model's body has been the bearer of symbolic values. The naked body is anything but value-neutral. This was clear from as far back as Genesis, where nakedness – when Adam and

Eve, after having eaten of the Tree of Knowledge, understand that they actually are naked – is linked to shame. So they first cover themselves with fig-leaves, before God creates coats of skins to clothe them with (Genesis 3:7, 21).

What a naked body *means* varies enormously: in ancient Greece, slaves and athletes went naked without this being particularly sensational, and public nudity, according to the cultural theorist Norbert Elias, was fairly unproblematic during the sixteenth century, after which a kind of shame boundary was established, requiring the body always to be clothed in situations where it was visible to others.[15] In recent times this shame boundary has once more become looser in large sections of the Western world. So the philosopher Mario Perniola goes a bit too far when he claims that clothes give people their anthropological, social and religious identity – in short, their 'being' – and that nakedness is to be understood as a privation, a lack.[16] This represents far too sharp a division between the naked and the clothed body; rather there is nothing that can be called a completely 'naked' body, as the naked body will always be 'clothed' because of its social definitions. And the more meaning that is ascribed to clothing, the more meaning will its visible absence have.[17] If you remove all the clothes, you will not find a 'natural' body but a body that is shaped by fashion: the body is no more 'natural' than the clothes it wears.[18]

Clothes fashions are often presented as a kind of disguise, as something that conceals the true nature of a person or a body.[19] Against this view I would argue that there is no such thing as a 'true nature'. What is considered as 'nature' is culture-related to a very great extent. Furthermore, why should this 'nature', of all things, be 'truer' than anything else? Baudelaire emphasizes fashion as a symptom of man's yearning to approach an ideal by going beyond what is given by nature:

> Fashion should thus be considered as a symptom of the taste for the ideal which floats on the surface of all the crude, terrestrial and loathsome bric-à-brac that the natural life accumulates in the human brain: as sublime deformation of Nature, or rather a permanent and repeated attempt at her *reformation*.[20]

Baudelaire stresses the dandy as an ideal that is opposed to the natural – the beauty of the dandy is anti-natural.[21] He does not find a norm by looking out into nature: 'The Dandy should aspire to be uninterruptedly sublime. He should live and sleep in front of the mirror.'[22] In relation to the art of make-up, Baudelaire claims that its task should not at all be to 'imitate' nature. The point is rather to 'surpass nature'. And if it does so explicitly, it becomes true: 'Maquillage has no need to hide itself or to shrink from being suspected; on the contrary, let it display itself, at least if it does so with frankness and honesty.'[23] Rather than use nature as a norm, as in pre-modern aesthetics, it is a question of establishing one's own norm. Rather than a disguise, the way we dress and otherwise adorn ourselves ought to be thought of as an active technique for the presentation of our physical self. Here it is possible to glean something from Thomas Carlyle's *Sartor Resartus*. For Carlyle, clothes are crucial to man's humanity, and he rejects the idea of an original natural state of *naked* perfection.[24] All in all, the distinction between 'fashion' and 'nature' is dubious for, as Simmel points out: 'the life-form of fashion is natural for man as a social being.'[25]

If life really is a beauty competition, as the fashion designer Thierry Mugler has claimed,[26] one must hope to have been born at a time when the norms of beauty happen to correspond to one's natural features. According to Robert Musil:

> There are, of course, in all periods all kinds of countenances, but only one type will be singled by a period's

> taste as its ideal image of happiness and beauty while all the other faces do their best to copy it, and with the help of fashion and hairdressers even the ugly ones manage to approximate the ideal. But there are some faces that never succeed, faces born to a strange distinction of their own, unyieldingly expressing the regal and banished ideal beauty of an earlier period.[27]

We live in an age, however, when the unhappy souls born with the ideal of beauty of another age have a greater opportunity than ever before of being able to fit in with their own age. There are limits to how much a body can be modified via cosmetics, hairstyles and training, but by intervening more directly via cosmetic surgery (removing a little here and adding a little there) the ideal of beauty that applies at any given time can apparently be brought within the reach of more and more people.

Cosmetic surgery is mushrooming as an industry. Even in Norway, a country with a population of about 4.6 million, it was estimated in 2004 that about 80,000 Norwegian women have undergone cosmetic surgery and about 250,000 more say that they are contemplating it.[28] That is far from 'all women', but it is a considerable number, one that is rising sharply from year to year. This is not just affecting women, either. Karl Kraus's aphorism that 'Cosmetics is the study of the female cosmos'[29] has become increasingly applicable to men. Today's man is placed in a world where his external appearance, towards which he has a reflective attitude, is becoming of crucial importance to how he views himself. One recent study claims that 43 per cent of all men in the US are dissatisfied with their appearance – three times as many as 25 years ago.[30] More and more men are modifying their appearance by cosmetic surgery.

We have definitely seen a normalization of cosmetic surgery, which enables an adaptation to a norm over and above what can be achieved by the body's own work on itself.[31] A fascinating case in this connection is the French performance artist Orlan, whose work is herself. From 1990 she was engaged on the *Reincarnation of St Orlan*, which required her to undergo a series of plastic surgery operations and thereby recreate herself using features taken from works of art, such as the chin from Botticelli's *Venus* and the eyes of Boucher's *Europa*. Most people who undergo cosmetic surgery do so with far less radical intent, but the basic principle is the same – to reform the body to correspond to a given ideal. Cosmetic surgery is only a radicalization of earlier forms of body modification: there is only a difference of degree between having a haircut and having liposuction or a silicone implant. Other forms of body modification, such as piercing, tattooing and scar decoration, also became highly popular in the 1990s. Like all other fashions, however, the trend died away when the fashion became too widespread.[32] Tattoos, however, are a paradoxical fashion phenomenon. Their relative permanence ought initially to make them rather ill-suited as a fashion, since it is not possible simply to get rid of them when the fashion is over. This brings us to an interesting point. Various forms of body decoration (from make-up to more radical body modifications) are found in all cultures, but generally speaking these play a group-identifying role in non-Western societies. In our modern Western societies, however, they are on the contrary interpreted as an assertion of individuality.[33]

According to Harold Koda, a curator at the Metropolitan Museum of Art: 'Fashion is the evidence of the human impulse to bring the body closer to an elusive transient ideal'.[34] As the fashion theorist Valerie Steele has remarked, the corset never really disappeared; it was rather converted into other types of underwear and finally into the well-trained modern body.[35] Jean Paul Gaultier's corsets, which were to be worn on top of the clothes rather than underneath them, were a clear comment on this. The hard shapes of the corset were no longer to keep human fat in – and the hard surface was rather just an expression of a body that had become hard. Is one free of the corset when one no longer shapes the body by means of it and has shaped it instead by realizing the same norm via endless hours in a keep-fit studio or gym? The hours spent in the gym and the intervention of the plastic surgeon are not seen as imposed on the individual from the outside. Apparently, one freely chooses to replace fat by muscle and to submit to the surgeon's scalpel. At the same time it is obvious that this free choice is not unqualified at all but takes place on the basis of an internalization of social norms.

Baudrillard writes: 'Like dieting, body-building, and so many other things, jogging is a new form of voluntary servitude.'[36] The disciplinary power that most people are affected by is not that exercised behind prison walls, but is that exerted via television, newspapers, magazines and the media, which present us with an ideal for the physical self that will always be out of reach for almost everybody. The body becomes something that will always fall short. The ideal constantly changes, usually becoming more extreme, so that anyone who happens to achieve a body ideal will soon have fallen short of the next one. Even models fall short of the norms: as far back as the 1950s it was not unusual for some to undergo cosmetic surgery in order to approach the norm, for example by removing the back molars in order to achieve hollow cheeks, or by having ribs removed in order to get the right body shape. The discrepancy between models' bodies and 'normal' bodies continues to increase. Today, the average American model weighs 23 per cent less than the average American woman, whereas only a generation ago the difference was 8 per cent.[37] The models are closest to the norm, but even their bodies, which are quite extreme to start with, are further modified by computerized image manipulation. In this way, the norm becomes pure fiction, but does not lose its normative function because of that.

The sociologist Anthony Giddens draws attention to how the body is becoming increasingly 'reflexively mobilised', that rather then being something 'given', it is subjected to 'fashioning' work.[38] All physical skills such as walking, smiling and swimming are technical and social. Walking is not purely instinctive and value-neutral in human beings – it is learned in a social field and expresses different values. There is a considerable difference between the gait of a slacker and a regular officer. The way one walks is socially formed, and there is no completely 'natural' way of walking, even though some certainly seem to be more exaggerated than others. Not only is the body saturated in social norms when in activity, it is so at rest as well.

With the exception of extreme practices such as feet-binding, we can hardly claim that one fashion is more 'natural' than another, since what can be seen as 'natural' is just as changeable as fashion itself. When we look at portraits of women from the late medieval period they often seem bizarre, to put it mildly. They have a very short, slim upper body topped by a large head and then, beneath two tiny breasts, there is an amply curved, though fairly unshapely, lower body that almost looks like some huge plinth for the small upper body. But that seemed 'natural' to people at the time. The late Gothic period's swelling bellies seem strange to us, and in the latter sixteenth century there would seem to be no limits as to how large a stomach a woman could have and yet still be attractive. On the contrary, it would seem that the norm was the bigger the better. It must be pointed out, however, that a toned 'hardbody' from the 1980s would have seemed weird to someone from the late Gothic period. In the early seventeenth century Rubens would hardly have been impressed by Kate Moss's body, and the typical Rubens model would never be let loose on a cat-walk nowadays, as presumably she would be at least ten sizes too big. One ideal of beauty that is quite unique to our age is visible bones. A constant feature of all ideals of beauty until the First World War was that a beautiful body had to have enough fat and muscle for the skeleton to remain hidden beneath them. Visible ribs and hips were 'unnatural' and ugly. The ideology of beauty normally operates with an idea of something 'natural', but the 'natural' body is, historically and socially speaking, an extremely variable entity. It must be pointed out that there have also been periods, such as during the later seventeenth century and the eighteenth, when the 'artificial' was approved fashion, but the crucial thing is that both 'natural' and 'artificial' ideals are constructs that change over time.

'Nature' has never been a guide when it comes to ideal bodies, even though each age has a tendency to regard its own ideal as being 'the natural'. What is a 'natural' position for the waist? In the seventeenth century the waist moved down to what we now regard its 'natural' position, but it has moved up and down quite a lot since then. Even if we confine ourselves to the twentieth century, we can see that it has moved between the hips and the breasts. Where the 'natural' position of the waist is would seem to be something that is completely a matter of convention. Changes in ideal bodies can be seen from display dummies. In the early twentieth century they had relatively strong shoulders and upper arms while the waist was slender (the classic hour-glass figure), with breasts protruding forwards and posterior backwards. Dummies of the 1920s, on the other hand, are characterized by a much slimmer figure, although collar bones or distinct muscles are not visible until the 1930s, which had a slimmer ideal body than any previous time in history. After the Second World War breasts and hips become larger again, whereas those of the 1960s have a more androgynous and angular figure. In the 1970s the most important development is that the dummies also display features of people from other parts of the world, but even so the ideal remains slim and youthful – a trend that has lasted until the present day. It should also be pointed out that not only the female body has been subject to the cultural conventions that prevail at any given time and adjust the relationships between the various parts of the body. Men too have had to adapt to the prevailing norms, for example by wearing a corset, but the results have normally been less radical than demanded of women. The ideals for the male body have mainly been linked to the size of the shoulders, hips and stomach. There has normally been a connection between the ideal bodies for both sexes, with a generous stomach or a slim waist being the approved norm for both sexes at the same time. When breasts are emphasized in women, however, the tendency has been for men's shoulders to become broader.

Are there 'natural' reasons for men and women wearing different clothes? Before the fourteenth century the differences between clothing for men and women are relatively small, but after that point the shape of clothes tends to be related to gender, with women wearing dresses that were admittedly more body-hugging than clothes worn previously, while men began to wear tights with short trousers worn over them. The idea that men's and women's bodies are basically similar, but that a woman's body – especially the genitals – is less developed than a man's, was not abandoned until the seventeenth century. In the course of the following century, however, it became increasingly usual to consider men and women as basically different with regards both physical and mental characteristics. The philosopher Jean-Jacques Rousseau is a typical example of this way of thinking. Men's and women's fashions also became correspondingly divergent. What is cause and what is effect, to what extent changes in the view of gender influenced fashion, or vice versa, is difficult to decide. It is most likely that the changes in clothes fashions and the view of gender tended to reinforce each other.

Trousers are a good example of what Roland Barthes calls a 'mythologization' (i.e. naturalization), by which a completely contingent definition is raised to the status of a natural law. There is no physiological reason for trousers being a specifically male garment. In nineteenth-century France women were actually forbidden to wear trousers, although working-class women in particular broke this prohibition. Knickers were also highly suspect, as the separation of a woman's thighs, even by a small piece of fabric, was considered directly obscene. Girls could wear knickers until puberty, but not subsequently, as the only adult women who wore them were prostitutes. Various attempts to introduce knickers were made in the mid-nineteenth century. American feminists were among those who began to wear loose pantaloons gathered at the ankle, known as bloomers. These were named after Amelia Bloomer, who designed and wore them in public about 1850. The pioneers were forced to abandon the attempt because they were ridiculed to such an extent that they became a liability to the American feminist movement. The invention and spread of the bicycle, however, which was well established by the 1890s, made it sensible for women to wear trousers, since it was highly impractical to cycle wearing a skirt. At first a kind of divided skirt was worn, but gradually this gave way to normal trousers. From the 1920s and '30s it became more usual for women to wear trousers (both long and short) for sport and leisure activities. Yet, even so, several decades were to pass before a woman wearing trousers could go to the office or to a party without attracting negative attention.

Once women began to show their legs in the twentieth century these became the most erotic part of the body. There are considerable historical variations when it comes to which part of the body is considered particularly attractive, this being reflected in their being emphasized or covered by clothes.[39] There are also variations when it comes to what skin colour is considered attractive. Before the 1920s a brown skin colour was thought vulgar by prosperous white people, because this colour was linked to physical labour in the sun. In the 1920s, however, rich Americans began to take their holidays on the French Riviera and it soon became fashionable to be tanned.[40] Over the past few decades a strong tan has become somewhat less fashionable, perhaps because 'everybody' could now afford holidays down south, perhaps following health scares. Generally speaking, though, it is now difficult to say that any particular skin colour is the single norm.

A part of the body that has undergone interesting transformations in the name of fashion is the female breast.[41] It was not until the mid-fifteenth century that clothes were developed that made it obvious that women actually have breasts and partially drew attention to this fact, although it was well disguised. Two centuries were to pass before full breasts were presented as attractive. Before that time large breasts were thought of as common and vulgar – absolutely not something for the higher echelons of society, which was normative.[42] Ideal breasts became larger during the seventeenth century before decreasing once more in the eighteenth century, assuming an apple-like shape that was retained as the standard until the end of the nineteenth century, when ideal breasts once more became fuller and more central for 'femininity'. The ideal size of breasts varied considerably during the twentieth century. It is remarkable how little the development of the ideal breast has corresponded to the ideal body in general. The 'natural' thing would be for a slender body to have small breasts and an ampler ideal body to have large breasts, since despite everything there is a certain correlation between the size of breasts and the amount of body fat elsewhere. But the exact opposite would seem to have been the case: ample bodies have had small breasts and slim bodies have had relatively large breasts – as is the case today.

What is 'beautiful', what would represent a deviation from a beauty norm and what role such a deviation plays are all relative when it comes to time and place.[43] If one searches for universal ideals of beauty, one is liable to emerge empty-handed.[44] Apart from symmetrical features having been, generally speaking, considered attractive and asymmetrical ones the opposite, it is very difficult to find any universal 'beautiful' qualities. Symmetry can be found in many variants: both slender and ample bodies can be symmetrical, small and large eyes, long and short legs, narrow and wide shoulders. Even so, symmetry is generally a central feature. Not least because of this, Rei Kawakubo's experiments with asymmetrical shapes have been thought-provoking. These items rewrite the body, and she is reported as saying that in her work 'the body becomes dress becomes body'.[45] The human figure when wearing these clothes looks distorted, and yet beautiful, so that Kawakubo would thereby seem to be questioning symmetry as a necessary ingredient of the ideal of beauty. Kawakubo creates clothes that seem 'unnatural' to a Western gaze, because they have not been created in accordance with Western conventions, but this also makes clear to what extent our way of looking is determined by these conventions, since we see that they could have been different.

6

Fashion and Art

There you are
at another preview
In a pose
the artist and you
To look so loud
may be considered tacky
Collectors wear black clothes
by Issey Miyake.
Pet Shop Boys[1]

The eighteenth-century separation of arts from crafts placed tailoring very much in the latter category. Clothes were placed in an extra-artistic sphere – where, for the most part, they have remained. Ever since *haute couture* was introduced around 1860, fashion has aspired to be recognized as fully fledged art. This was clearly the case with Charles Frederick Worth and Paul Poiret. Worth's career promoted the 'emancipation' of the fashion designer from being a simple craftsman, completely subject to the wishes of the customer, to being a 'free creator' who, in accordance with the Romantic view of art, created works on the basis of his or her own subjectivity. Worth, who opened his fashion house in Paris in 1857, was the first real 'king of fashion'. He chose the fabrics, developed a design and produced the garment. It was with Worth that fashion designers also began to 'sign' their clothes, as did artists, by inserting a tag. In actual fact this freedom was rather restricted, as the creations had to appeal to the aesthetic preferences of the customer – and the customer would refuse to pay for clothes that could not be worn. This in turn means that the creations were not allowed to remove themselves too far from any style prevalent at the time. Despite this, it was Worth who initiated the struggle for the clothes designer to be recognized as an artist on a par with other artists. He consciously dressed 'artistically', collected art and antiques and engaged such recognized photographers as Félix Nadar to take his portrait.[2] The urge to achieve artistic recognition by collecting and organizing art exhibitions was typical to an even greater degree of Paul Poiret, who in 1913 stated categorically: 'I am an artist, not a dressmaker.'[3] He also began giving his creations such titles as 'Magyar' and 'Byzantine' instead of the numbers that had been used until then, presumably to add an extra symbolic dimension to his garments.

Fashion designers have never managed to gain total recognition as artists, but they continue to strive so to do. One of the most striking examples of this urge is the emergence of 'conceptual clothes' in the 1980s. One widespread strategy was to turn traditions 'inside-out', as when Gaultier designed his famous corset that was to be worn on top of other clothes, and Helmut Lang made his dresses with shoulder-pads on the outside of the dress. Among the more moderate modifications of norms, mention should be made of Comme des Garçons' shirts with two collars and buttons of various sizes, which violate the conventions of what a shirt 'must' look like. Many garments were designed with seams on the outside, which can be compared to the trend in modern art to accentuate the materiality of the work, for example by marking the pencil strokes clearly in the paintings. In the 1980s Rei Kawakubo began to create fabrics with 'faults' by 'sabotaging' the machines producing them, after which she allowed the fabrics to be exposed to wind and weather for days on end.

Many fashion designers have used strategies normally associated with contemporary art rather than the world of fashion, by creating clothes that are better suited to exhibitions in galleries and museums than for actual wear. Hussein Chalayan's shows often seemed more like art installations than fashion shows. At a 1994 show, for example, the clothes were accompanied by a text that gave an account of how they came into being, and of how they had been buried underground for weeks before being dug up and shown on the catwalk. He has claimed, with some justification, that many of his creations would do better on a museum wall than on a human body. The display of clothes at fashion shows has to a great extent systematically broken with the spectators' expectations, as when Martin Margiela removed the cat-walk and showed a collection in utter darkness, only lit by umbrellas carried by 'fashion assistants' in white coats, or when he showed only clothes on posters carried round by not very glamorous 'models'. On one occasion he decided not to show any clothes at all. He designed clothes from lining material with seams on the outside and loose threads. The label, that essential part of every fashion item worthy of the name, shaped like a white square without any text, appeared to have been put on carelessly so that it had to be removed in order not to create creases in the garment. For 2001 he made a collection in size 74, which is far too large for anyone but giants, and in doing so put the spotlight on the standardization of the body in the fashion industry. Despite this he insists that fashion is a craft, not art.[4] But the way his creations are presented indicate that they are precisely to be considered as art. From that point of view, Issey Miyake's insistence that he makes *art* and not fashions seems more credible.

These clothes were not made only to be clothes-as-art but were also to function as an investment in a brand name, so as to generate income. Dissociating oneself from the market has always been an important strategy for increasing cultural capital, but the aim of increasing the cultural capital of fashion is normally then to use this in order to increase the financial capital. Fashion has always found itself in a space between art and capital, where it has often embraced the cultural side in order to tone down its financial side. Rei Kawakubo's Comme des Garçons is, despite all its avant-garde aesthetics, a business with a turnover of more than a hundred million dollars a year. No matter how ingenious fashion advertisements become, they are still advertisements. Fashion magazines, however, are designed in such a way that it is becoming increasingly difficult to distinguish between editorial material, artistic contributions and advertising. The amount of advertising has increased dramatically and now takes up about three times as many pages as the editorial material in a normal edition of *Vogue*, yet it is presented in such a way that it can be difficult to spot that it is actually advertising. And since there is hardly such a thing as 'critical fashion journalism', it is difficult to consider the editorial material as being anything other than advertising. An important reason for fashion not having attained the same recognition as other forms of art is that there are traditions for serious criticism within the visual arts, music, literature and film, while this is almost totally absent from fashion.[5] The press is crucial for 'creating the creators', as Bourdieu puts it.[6] This of course applies to all forms of journalism, and Bourdieu points out that it is the task of critics and journalists to produce a belief in the objects in the fields they write about. In turn this strengthens their own position. This is extremely obvious in fashion journalism, which struggles for credibility through having a tendency to be far too uncritical. The links between the press and the industry are so close that it is difficult to consider the fashion press as anything other than the extended arm of the fashion houses.

As far back as the time of Paul Poiret, art was used to increase the cultural capital of the designer.[7] Coco Chanel, for example, spent much time cultivating contacts with known artists, supported dance performances and organized magnificent dinner parties with the 'right' guests to increase her cultural capital. She was a friend of Picasso and Stravinsky, and created clothes for Cocteau and Diaghilev. The rapprochement between the fashion industry and the field of art experienced a strong upswing in the 1980s and '90s. The fashion houses employed well-known artists to increase their artistic credibility, as when Cindy Sherman took fashion photos for Comme des Garçons and Nan Goldin for Helmut Lang and Matsuda. This was not a completely new phenomenon: Man Ray, for example, took fashion photographs. Tracey Emin has devised advertising for Vivienne Westwood. Helmut Lang installed Jenny Holzer's neon sign in his New York shop, Julian Schnabel was an interior designer for Azzedine Alaïa, and Issey Miyake let Frank Gehry design shop interiors. Hugo Boss has established an art prize that is awarded in collaboration with the Guggenheim Museum, and Calvin Klein has sponsored a number of exhibitions, while Gucci has sponsored the sculptor Richard Serra and the performance artist Vanessa Beecroft.

Fashion houses such as Prada and Cartier have gone further than the traditional role of art patrons and established their own museums. Most of the large fashion houses sponsor museums of contemporary art, so as to gain closer ties with the art world, and sometimes they are rewarded with exhibitions at precisely these institutions, which apparently have a 'magical' ability to transform ordinary objects into something higher: 'art'. Since the Metropolitan Museum of Art held an Yves Saint-Laurent exhibition in 1983 (although in the costume department), there has been a stream of exhibitions on art and fashion.[8] In 1997 Versace had an exhibition at the Metropolitan Museum of Art, and in 2000 the Guggenheim in New York had its greatest public success ever with an Armani exhibition, which then continued to Bilbao, Berlin, London,

Rome and Las Vegas. Giorgio Armani said at the opening that he was proud to have been chosen to 'stand next to works by the most influential artists of the 20th century', though he omitted to mention the generous sum he had donated to the Guggenheim in sponsorship money. This exhibition was the subject of much sharp criticism, partly because, rather than being a retrospective exhibition of Armani's best-known creations, it mainly emphasized his most recent collections, so that many people felt he had bought himself a commercial spot at the Guggenheim. The thought behind the efforts made by fashion houses to gain access to art institutions is not least that these institutions possess heavy symbolic values one would like a share of. If one wishes to add symbolic value to an object, one of the simplest ways of doing so is to place the object alongside other objects that have such a large symbolic value, because such value is 'contagious'. But it also happens that the object that passes on such symbolic value to another loses some of its own value in the process, and this has been behind much of the criticism of fashion having been allowed to slip inside the art institutions. Notwithstanding this, the special symbolic value of art in the modern world is one of the reasons why it is used so much in advertising contexts.[9]

In the 1920s fashion was abreast of art and architecture when it came to being 'modern'. The straight, flat-chested look of women's fashion was completely in accord with the treatment of lines and surfaces in Cubist art produced at the same time by such painters as Léger and Braque. It was a fashion that renounced ornament in favour of the pure cultivation of form and as such was a striking example of a modernist *ethos*. Chanel made a radical move by basing her creations for women on men's clothing rather than relying on previous women's fashions and 'exotic' touches. This move matched the general trend of the time towards simpler forms. Chanel was admittedly by no means the only one to create such simple clothes – at sky-high prices – but she managed to market this as *her* style, despite the fact that many other fashion designers were making similar clothes. While Chanel represented the functionalist side of modernism, Elsa Schiaparelli turned towards Surrealism and collaborated with Salvador Dalí to incorporate fashion into the Surrealist movement. Schiaparelli started to use new materials such as cellophane and glass, created hats shaped like shoes and employed colours that were usually considered ugly – not least shocking pink. She was probably the first fashion designer who was really part of the avant-garde, and she was a pioneer of later avant-garde strategies in fashion, such as how to decontextualize and recontextualize objects, to mix 'high' and 'low', and to use unexpected shades and materials.

At the beginning of the twentieth century it was not unusual for visual artists also to design clothes. In 1906, for example, Gustav Klimt photographed his close friend Emilie Flöge, the fashion designer, modelling ten dresses that he had created. Others who tried their hand included Henri Matisse, Salvador Dalí, Aleksandr Rodchenko, Sonia Delaunay, Natal'ya Goncharova and Oscar Schlemmer. Yves Saint-Laurent made a collection in 1965 inspired by Mondrian, with the characteristic rectangular patterns in bright colours and broad black lines. He continued to make dresses related to paintings by, among others, Andy Warhol and Roy Lichtenstein – as well as a Picasso skirt. Shortly afterwards Warhol made a paper dress for which he recycled his own soup can motif, and Lichtenstein made shirts. Pop art and fashion seemed to be made for each other. Pursuing this idea, a number of artists, including Jenny Holzer and Keith Haring, produced T-shirts to bring art out onto the street during *Documenta VII* in 1982. At the same time there were a number of examples of the opposite, as certain artistic expressions, such as Jenny Holzer and Barbara Kruger's use of 'slogan art', were now placed in fashion contexts, for example in Katherine Hamnett's collections.[10] Just as art was used in fashion, so was fashion also used in art, as when Cindy Sherman used clothes from Gaultier in *Untitled #131* (1983).

In the course of the twentieth century art and fashion have been like two neighbours who sometimes happily rub shoulders and who at other times cannot stand the sight of each other. Or it would perhaps be more precise to say that there has been an asymmetry in this neighbourliness, since fashion has always wanted to be loved by art, while art has been more ambivalent, sometimes embracing fashion only to thrust it away again.[11] The art of the 1960s, pop art in particular, generally looked favourably at fashion. After about 1960 total absorption within a single medium, in the manner championed by the abstract expressionists, no longer seemed to produce results worthy of interest. It could be said that the artistic process whereby each individual form of art should primarily research its own idiom had been completed. It seemed obvious that art ought to focus its attention on the world around it once more, and fashion offered itself as an area for artistic research. The art of the politicized 1970s, on the other hand, was quite hostile to fashion, which was viewed as an indicator of the capitalist world's squalor, the false consciousness of the masses and the suppression of women in a world controlled by masculine values. Since the 1980s, however, fashion has once more been accepted by art, which has been more willing to absorb consumer culture. The least we can say is that over the past couple of decades art has been more ambivalent towards fashion, whereas during the 1970s it was unambiguously dismissive.

An important moment in the mutual rapprochement between fashion and art took place in February 1982, when the cover of the influential American magazine *Artforum* showed a model wearing an evening dress designed by Issey Miyake. It was not unusual for fashion clothes and photos to be used in an artistic context, but what distinguished this cover photo from the common *use* of fashion in art was that this dress was presented as something that *in itself* was art. In other words, it was an indication that the old dream of fashion designers was in the process of being realized. During the 1980s and '90s it became increasingly more usual for serious magazines such as *Artforum* and *Flash Art* to mention fashion designers like Miyake, Kawakubo and Margiela, while fashion houses at the same time took to advertising more in the various magazines. Comme des Garçons produced its own magazine, which caused one critic to remark: 'The clothing it [Comme des Garçons] manufactures and markets is like art in every respect except being art. And now it has created one of the great art magazines of our time, except that it's not really an art magazine, it's a clothing catalogue.'[12] This critic assumes there is a very sharp dividing line between art and fashion, but the quotation underlines, despite this, how strongly interwoven the two areas had become. Fashion has approached art and art fashion in such a way that it has become difficult to make any clear distinction between the two. For the January 2000 issue of *Vogue* a number of the most prominent young British artists, including Tracey Emin, Marc Quinn and the Chapman brothers, made portraits and sculptures of Kate Moss, the result being at least on a par with what is on display in museums of contemporary art.

The most 'artistic' aspect of fashion is normally linked to its display. Paul Poiret was the first designer to turn the fashion show into an impressive social event, and Jean Patou developed this further; but they could scarcely have imagined how fashion shows would develop towards the end of the century. During the 1980s and '90s fashion shows became ever more spectacular and were located in ever more imaginative arenas, as when John Galliano took a football stadium and turned it into a fairytale forest. The standard was set when, for the showing of his autumn/winter collection of 1984–5, Thierry Mugler wanted to recreate the virgin birth on a catwalk full of nuns and cherubs, with the finale marked by a model descending from heaven in a cloud of smoke and cascades of pink confetti. At the time Mugler was criticized for letting the show completely overshadow the clothes, but soon such fashion shows were the rule rather than the exception.[13] They were large and extravagant in order to create maximum publicity, and it became clear that *haute couture* had become part of the entertainment industry.[14] An obvious example of this was that tickets to Mugler's fashion show were sold to 'ordinary' people – in addition to the press, buyers and other invited persons – making a total of 6,000 spectators. *Haute couture* is, to put it mildly, unprofitable if understood as the production of clothing for sale, but as an advertising strategy it is far more profitable. Central to these shows were the super-models. Worth was the first fashion designer to use living mannequins to present his clothes, but he could hardly have imagined that a time would come when the super-models who showed off the clothes would completely overshadow them. Right up until the early 1980s there was a distinction between cat-walk models and photo models. The cat-walk models had bodies that fitted the clothes to be on show, but not necessarily faces that were equally attractive. When fashion shows developed to the point where it was basically no longer a question of presenting clothes but rather of lending glamour to the brand name, the photo models took over the cat-walk.

Recent fashion has not, however, devoted itself exclusively to glamour. The fashions of the 1990s in particular tended towards aggression, violence, destruction and dirt.[15] One of the more extreme shows was Rei Kawakubo's stunt for the premiere of the 1995 spring collection of Comme des Garçons. This was held on the fiftieth anniversary of the liberation of Auschwitz, with models with razed heads taking to the cat-walk wearing striped pyjamas that bore a striking resemblance to prison uniforms.[16] It was hardly a mere coincidence, even though Kawakubo insisted it was precisely that (and immediately afterwards recalled the garments), and naturally it caused an outcry. But it also proved that not all advertising is good advertising. Even so, it is clear that this turning away from glamour towards shock-effects was a repetition of a far older trend in modernist art. In *The Work of Art in the Age of Mechanical Reproduction* (1936) Walter Benjamin claimed that the essence of art had been radically transformed by the technical possibilities of reproduction.[17] While a work of art had traditionally been characterized by its uniqueness, since there was only one copy in existence, it had now become reproducible. According to Benjamin, the 'aura' of the work of art is threatened by reproducibility, because its uniqueness is replaced by its appearance *en masse*. But rather than mourn the loss of aura, he claims that this opens up new progressive potential. The loss of aura does not mean that the aesthetic experience is lost, rather that it changes its nature and abandons the beautiful. The aesthetic experience now has to be liberated by the *shock*, he claims. And, as we know, shock strategies became a central element in modernist art, with the works of the Vienna actionists in the 1960s and 1970s as a high-point. It is possible to see an analogy here with fashion, where unique originals (*haute couture*) are replaced by an infinite number of reproducible 'copies' (*prêt-à-porter*). But what are actually bought and sold are the *prêt-à-porter* collections, and these too have to be aesthetically interesting. The solution lay in trying to uphold the aura of *haute couture*, and by pretending that this aura, via the brand name, was inherited by the *prêt-à-porter* collections. Whether the aura could be maintained in *haute couture* and passed on to *prêt-à-porter* is, however, doubtful. Perhaps that is the reason why fashion abandoned the aesthetic of beauty so much at the end of the twentieth century, and presumptively controversial designers such as Alexander McQueen became so central.

McQueen's collections have had titles like *Highland Rape* and *The Golden Shower* and to a great extent have embraced an avant-garde aesthetic. These collections almost cry out that they are ART and not something as trivial as 'normal' clothes. (The artistic integrity, however, does not go any deeper than *The Golden Shower* being renamed *Untitled* when McQueen's sponsor, American Express, protested against the title's sexual connotations.)[18] The showing of *Highland Rape* was strongly criticized for speculating in sexualized violence, but McQueen himself claimed that he wished to draw attention to and criticize the rape of the Scottish highlands by the British in the eighteenth century.[19] The main character of McQueen's second collection for Givenchy, *Eclect Dissect* (summer 1997), was a surgeon and collector who, at the transition of the eighteenth century into the nineteenth, travelled round the world and collected exotic objects, including women, to dissect them and put them back together again in his laboratory. The then popular theme of 'the serial killer', featured in a host of cinema films, was linked to Victorian fashions. It was in many ways a successful performance, aesthetically speaking – for it was a performance more than anything else – yet at the same time it gave the impression of trying a little too hard to be art rather than a traditional fashion show. McQueen has claimed that he is first and foremost interested in getting a reaction from the audience, and that he would rather have a show induce nausea than just be a pleasant cocktail party.[20] This is undoubtedly an artistic avant-garde pose. But if one places *Highland Rape* and *Eclect Dissect* in an art context, it very much loses its bite. The aesthetics of transgression had already been taken so far in art that these shows would scarcely have led to any noteworthy reactions in a purely art context. The reason why these shows commanded such great attention was precisely because they were *fashion* shows and the shock effect would hardly have been capable of being transferred to an art context. The same applies to the fashion show directed by the master of horror films Dario Argento for Trussardi in 1986, where the models were apparently murdered with a knife and dragged off the stage.

Towards the end of the twentieth century fashion seemed to have to pretend to be avant-garde in order to sell to the masses, even though an avant-garde for the masses might seem to be a contradiction in terms. In order to gain attention, fashion embraced the diametric opposite of what it had traditionally been associated with, covering glamour with dirt. The result was 'heroin chic', which in practice became an unwilling parody of street style. This fashion trend was brilliantly parodied in Ben Stiller's film *Zoolander* (2001), where the evil fashion guru Mugatu (Will Ferrell) presents the collection *Derelicte*, which he claims is 'the future of fashion' and which is inspired by 'the very homeless, the vagrants, the crack whores that make this wonderful city so unique'. This is more than a faint echo of Lacroix's statement to *Vogue* (April 1994): 'It's terrible to say, very often the most exciting outfits are from the poorest people.'[21]

This is the logical consequence of Yves Saint-Laurent's statement of 1968: 'Down with the Ritz – long live the street.' Here, Saint-Laurent was really knocking at a door long since flung open, since as early as the 1950s designers had dabbled in imitating the new street fashions that started with working-class teenagers and spread to young people from the middle and upper class. In fact, Chanel had already claimed that fashion only exists to the extent it makes an impact on the streets.[22] If this is the case, *haute couture* has not had a lot to do with fashion for some time. To an increasing extent *haute couture* has gained inspiration from the street, but this does not necessarily mean that it made an impact on the street scene because of that. According to Christian Lacroix: 'Even for *couture* we need an influence from real life, for you will kill *couture* if you restrict it to windows and museums.' But when 'the street' has been incorporated into *haute couture*, it costs hundreds of times as much by virtue of no longer being simply 'street style' but because – in some magical way or other – it has become transformed by a fashion designer. Dirt in the street is no longer ordinary dirt when it has been transformed by the alchemy of the designer. Dirt is merely decoration: it is never allowed to be really dirty. Futurists such as Giacomo Balla worked with fashion in order to break down the barrier between art and everyday life, but the part of fashion that has drawn closest to art is that which has removed itself as far as possible from everyday life. The fashion industry insists that fashion is something extraordinary, something beyond the consumer items of everyday life. Even the fashion that gains inspiration from the street has to be extraordinary in some sense or other. It is neither from nor for everyday life.

According to Walter Benjamin, photography has a tendency to beautify its object, being able, for example, to transform poverty into an object of pleasure. He writes:

> The more far-reaching the crisis of the present social order, the more rigidly its individual components are locked together in their death struggle, the more has the creative – in its deepest essence a sport, by contradiction out of imitation – become a fetish, whose lineaments live only in the fitful illumination of changing fashion. The creative in photography is its capitulation to fashion. *The world is beautiful* – that is its watchword. Therein is unmasked the posture of a photography that can endow any soup can with cosmic significance but cannot grasp a single one of the human connexions in which it exists, even where most far-fetched subjects are more concerned with saleability than with insight.[23]

In the pictures of clothes in fashion photography there is, for example, no link between the garments and their origins, often in factories with underpaid workers.[24] The most horrendous working conditions can be turned into an object of pleasure. The photo detaches the object from its real relations and places it in a beautiful dream world.

In the 1990s 'reality' was one of the most fashionable things around. Fashion photographs had to be 'realistic' and show the models as 'real' people. Helmut Newton's and Guy Bourdin's photographs of the 1970s had a touch of cynical realism, but the realism of the 1990s went considerably further by removing most of what still remained of glamour in the fashion photograph.[25] Among the most extreme cases were Jean-Baptiste Mondino's photos in the June 1994 issue of *The Face*, which show models posing with pistols against their foreheads while blood drips from their lips. Themes such as violence, drugs, death and dirt were to mark 'the entrance of reality' into fashion. It is possible to claim, however, that it was rather because these themes had become so enormously widespread in popular culture, especially in films, where the themes have become completely fictionalized, that they could so easily be incorporated into fashion's play with surfaces. The fictionalization of our world has turned reality into a kind of commodity, but the reality that is for sale always turns out to be fictionalized. Fashion from this point of view is a realization of Baudrillard's assertion that the economy of the picture has replaced the being of 'reality'. The reality of fashion is always unreal.

We have ascertained that an increasingly active exchange between fashion and art has taken place, but have yet to answer the question: 'Is fashion art?' Anne Hollander states categorically: 'Dress is a form of visual art, a creation of images with the visible self as its medium.'[26] She does not, however, answer the question as to why clothes ought to be considered as art when traditionally they have been excluded from the domain of art. It would be a good idea to find a criterion that can decide to what extent fashion falls inside or outside the area of art, but it is doubtful if such can be found.

Suzy Menkes, fashion editor at *International Herald Tribune*, has written that: 'Genuine fashion must be functional and, therefore, can only be classified as applied art or craft.

If a garment is not wearable, it is not fashion. But it just might be art.'[27] That is a problematic point of view. She uses unusability as a criterion of demarcation between art and non-art. This is a traditional criterion found by such writers as Adorno.[28] It can be said to have been clearly formulated for the first time in Kant, who in his *Critique of Judgement* (1790) distinguishes between free and dependent beauty.[29] This distinction has to do with how far the aesthetic experience serves any particular purpose in an objective sense, that is whether it can be *used* for anything. Kant requires an object for aesthetic judgment to show an absence of purpose or end if it is to be a genuine object of art or, rather, to be the object of a purely aesthetic judgment. It ought by now to be clear that nearly all clothes have precisely such a purpose. They are *for* something: to be worn. There are, of course, examples of clothes that have been designed in such a way that they cannot be used, but these are exceptions. For that reason, clothes virtually disappear from such Kantian aesthetics. At the same time, it is obvious that the aesthetic field comprises a great deal more than the small group of objects capable of satisfying the Kantian requirements. Such a Kantian point of view is problematic partly because it finds a range of objects unusable that even so can scarcely be called art, and partly because some contemporary art explicitly attempts to be useful.[30] Looking at the way art has developed in recent times, unusability has become an unusable criterion for art.

The fashion designer Zandra Rhodes, for her part, argues that fashion is actually 'more relevant, more artistic' than the art that is produced nowadays, precisely because fashion dwells on a concept of beauty that art, broadly speaking, has lost interest in.[31] This is no less problematic a point of view than Menkes's. Rhodes assumes that genuine art must of necessity be focused on beauty, but this is a view that has been severely criticized in relation to art, literature and philosophical aesthetics over the past 150 to 200 years. Rhodes can hardly be said to have presented a single argument as to why beauty should be a privileged aesthetic category. Furthermore, sections of the contemporary avant-garde, the clothes Margiela sprayed with mould, for example, would not qualify, since dwelling on beauty can hardly be said to be a primary concern.

Nathalie Khan has a different approach. She claims that what makes works by, say, Margiela art rather than design is that they contain a reflexive comment on the actual fashion industry of which he himself is a part.[32] Such reflexivity is a common feature of much *haute couture* over the past decades, not least in a number of Belgian and Japanese fashion designers. Reflecting on one's own medium in such a way is closely related to the self-reflexiveness of modernistic art. This was the task of modernistic art, according to the art theorist Clement Greenberg, who claimed that the essence of modernism consists in every kind of art having to prove its distinctive identity, what is unique to it, in order to underline its 'absolute autonomy'.[33] Each art discipline must 'criticize' itself in order to separate the essential about this discipline, so that it gets closer to a realization of its being. It is not unreasonable to say that it is precisely such an investigation of clothes as a specific medium that has been carried out by some contemporary avant-garde fashion. On the other hand, it has to be conceded that fashion carried out this process of reflection many decades after modernistic art had completed the task – admittedly without arriving at any final result. Even the most artistically advanced clothes fashion lags behind when compared to art, and as such it fails to live up to its own ideals – to be innovative. Considered as art, fashion is simply not all that fashionable. Having said that, it must also be added that self-reflexiveness can hardly function as a necessary or sufficient criterion for inclusion in art. Firstly, there are a number of activities that are characterized by such a self-reflexiveness – a metaphilosophical investigation, for example – without it being reasonable because of that to classify all such activities as art. Secondly, it is obvious that much art produced does not have such self-reflexiveness as its primary task.

So it is easier to agree with Sung Bok Kim's assertion that fashion quite simply is art, because the concepts of fashion and art have been expanded to contain both of them.[34] The concept of art has expanded so radically over the past century that it is hard to think of any object or any event that cannot be incorporated into it; it is now impossible to draw any line between art and non-art.[35] From this point of view, the question 'Is fashion art?' is superfluous, or at least rather uninteresting. When we look back at the art and art discourse of the twentieth century we can see that, to a great extent, it kept returning to the question: 'Is *this* art?' This question has become superfluous, precisely because it always has to be answered in the affirmative, since asking the question as to whether something is art firmly anchors it in the world of art. Rather than asking whether something is art, we ought to ask the question as to what extent it is *good* or *relevant* art. We must consequently ask to what extent fashion, seen as art, is good art. It is more doubtful whether we can answer in the affirmative to any great extent.

In my opinion some examples of fashion have been absolutely on a par with contemporary art. I cannot see that Balenciaga's creations in the 1950s were any inferior to spatial experiments being explored in sculpture at the time. Schiaparelli's creations were probably just as advanced as most Surrealist pictorial art produced in the 1920s and '30s. Contemporary fashion designers have also carried out projects of high artistic quality. The spring/summer collection of Alexander McQueen in 2001 staged an interesting reflection on objectivization in fashion. A large rectangular box made of mirrors was placed on the cat-walk. The show deliberately began very late, so that the audience had to stare and stare at their own mirror-images for a long time, rather than consider the models. This move was particularly meaningful because the audience consisted to a great extent of fashion journalists, who earn their daily bread telling other people what they ought to look like. The observers had to objectify themselves. This process was then reversed when the show began, when it transpired that the box had been made in such a way that the models inside could not see the audience, only their own reflections. The audience could now observe the models without being seen themselves: they were present at a kind of peep-show. These are examples of fashion that are completely on a par with art, although most of what goes on is artistically uninteresting. Generally speaking, fashion – if it is to be considered art – is fairly insignificant art.

Can art learn anything from fashion? It can, at any rate, learn something about itself. Oscar Wilde writes that 'Of course there are fashions in art just as there are fashions in dress',[36] and one does not have to be a great art connoisseur to realize that this is true. There is no clear dividing line between art and fashion – we are not looking at two different worlds. This is not because fashion has 'gained' the level of art, but rather that practically everything (including art) is subject to the principles of fashion. The point is naturally not that art is fitfully attempting 'just' to be fashion – none of the areas of fashion has ever done that, whether clothes, art or philosophy – but rather that the *modus operandi* of fashion has become an increasingly crucial part of the development of this field.

Adorno claims that art is subject to an influence from fashion of which it is unaware:

> Despite the fact that it is manipulated commercially, fashion penetrates deep into works of art, and not simply by exploiting them. Discoveries such as Picasso's light painting are like transpositions of experiments from *haute couture* [. . .] Fashion is one of the figures that affect the historical movement of the sense apparatus

> and thereby, even if only to a minimal extent, features of the works of art that they conceal from themselves.[37]

While art often lives under the misapprehension of being raised above time, fashion has 'its truth as an unconscious consciousness of art's time-core'.[38] Art, like everything else, is subject to fashion, and precisely for that reason fashion contains such an 'unconscious consciousness' of the real conditions of art. At the same time, it must be pointed out that Adorno is critical, to put it mildly, of 'fashionable art', because fashion, in addition to administering a truth about art, also threatens the autonomy of art.[39] 'Art is not something pure that can be elevated above fashion,' he writes, but art at the same time has to 'resist fashion' if it is to be fully fledged art.[40] In other words, art must relate to fashion via a double movement, recognizing the power of fashion and that it is subject to fashion, and combating precisely that power. For Adorno, fashion is the greatest danger to culture, because it apparently homogenizes and thereby makes society more totalitarian. The task of art in relation to this is to become aware of the danger and to include reflection on the significance of fashion in itself. Art's relationship to fashion must thus be ambivalent – and it is not least such an ambivalence that has characterized research into fashion in artistic contexts over the past decades.

As Adorno sees it, art has to include reflection on how it is influenced by the temporality of fashion. If fashion is to become art, this also means that fashion-as-art has to reflect on how the art it is attempting to become a part of is influenced by fashion's own temporality. But here fashion fails on the whole, since it does not grasp that certain artistic projects have been dealt with, become unproductive or, if you like, 'gone out of fashion'. It is striking, for example, how much fashion – not least in the 1990s – kept returning to an avant-garde rhetoric that art had basically already abandoned.

In its attempt to be avant-garde, fashion has on the whole simply repeated empty gestures that had already been used up in the field of art. So it is ironic that artists over the last century have become increasingly preoccupied with fashion. In 1919 Max Ernst proclaimed: '*Fiat modes – pereat ars*' ('Long live fashion – may art perish').[41] It was meant to be an affirmation of the transient, as opposed to the eternal, where fashion was a model for art. The paradox is that art has continued to be in fashion, while fashion would basically seem to have gone out of fashion when it is to be considered as art. An important reason for art having remained in fashion could be that it actually manages to say something important from time to time, whereas fashion is caught in a loop where it mainly repeats itself and means increasingly less. It is hardly an exaggeration to say that today's fashion finds itself way down in a creative trough – and it is doubtful if it will come up again.

7

Fashion and Consumption

I'm all lost in the supermarket
I can no longer shop happily
I came in here for that special offer
A guaranteed personality
The Clash[1]

'Lucidity. Total lucidity, baby.'
'I wish I knew what that meant, Victor.'
'Three words, my friend: Prada, Prada, Prada.'
Bret Easton Ellis[2]

'Do you like them or not?'
'I like them if they're Lacroix.'
Absolutely Fabulous[3]

Our everyday lives have become increasingly commercialized, an ever greater number of commodities are in circulation, and more and more we are attempting to satisfy our needs and desires by consuming commodities and services.[4] What does it mean that we now live in a 'consumer society'? Earlier in the modern era we can say that we lived in a 'producer society', where citizens were mainly moulded to be producers. Their basic role was to produce. In postmodern society, this role has changed in that members of society are thought of rather as consumers.[5] This is the result of a lengthy process of development, and should not be taken to mean that formerly people were not consumers and that today they are not producers. Every society needs both producers and consumers. The change has to do with which role is the *primary* one. We can also include at this point the fact that we spend less and less of our lives working. The sociologist Manuel Castell has estimated that in Western Europe and North America we will soon be down to 30 working years in a life that lasts 75–80 years.[6] So we are producers for less than half our lives, while we are consumers throughout our lives.

Consumption culture is not a uniform phenomenon – it would be more accurate to talk about it in the plural, as a myriad of consumption cultures. Consumers are not a uniform group either, but there has been a tendency in much recent consumption theory to emphasize the 'postmodern' consumer.[7] Even though there would appear to be an ever increasing number of this type of consumer, there are a number of other types as well.[8] Every population displays a number of different patterns of consumption linked to such as geography, age and financial status.[9] Like the anthropologist Daniel Miller, I do not believe that any one single explanation can be found that is capable of accounting for the diversity of the consumption field.[10] There is, for example, 'altruistic' shopping, and Miller has criticized the widespread view of shopping as egoistic materialism on the basis of surveys of consumer behaviour.[11] He emphasizes that, on the contrary, love and concern for those nearest to us are crucial factors if one is to come up with a satisfactory explanation as to why and what people buy. That is a charming picture, and without a doubt it can shed light on some kinds of shopping, but most of what is bought is purchased by the individual consumer for himself or herself. An obvious reason for consuming is that certain necessities of life such as food and drink simply have to be satisfied, but this constitutes an ever decreasing amount of people's consumption. In classic liberal economic theories, the task of consumption is to satisfy already existing needs, but these theories will only be able to describe a limited amount of consumption. We do not only consume to cater for already existing needs: we do so probably just as much in order to create an identity. Additionally, consumption functions as a kind of entertainment.[12] It is an ever more usual means of combating boredom; as the sociologist Zygmunt Bauman writes: 'Not being bored – ever – is the norm of the consumers' life.'[13] I will make do with focusing on one aspect, but one which I consider to be of the essence: the symbolic dimension of consumption and the role this symbolic consumption allegedly plays in the formation of people's identity.

The anthropologists Mary Douglas and Baron Isherwood claim that 'commodities are neutral and the way in which they are used social: they can be used as barriers or bridges.'[14] There may be a reason for being sceptical about having a division between the commodity 'in itself' and its use. It should rather be said that use is a crucial part of what it means to be a particular commodity, but the most important thing is that commodities in use are not neutral. They have functions, and Douglas and Isherwood reduce these to two fundamental functions: bridges and barriers. They link people together or separate them from each other – like Simmel's 'socializing' and 'differentiating' forces. It is misleading to claim that commodities are used as barriers *or* bridges. If they are to have an identity-establishing function, the crucial thing is that they have both functions. A demarcation, for example that one does *not* dress like the majority, is insufficient to constitute an identity. There must also be a positive identification.[15] 'I am not a hippie' only provides a completely imprecise identity, one that has to be expanded by a positive identification, such as 'I am not a hippie because I am a punk rocker.' Social identity, in other words, calls for both a negative demarcation and a positive identification.

In chapter Three we dealt with a number of theories that claimed that consumption in general (and consumption of fashion in particular) ought to be explained on the basis of class differentiation. Gilles Lipovetsky rejects such models, which place a one-sided emphasis on consumption being controlled by ambitions of social recognition. In his opinion it is more motivated by a wish to experience well-being and pleasure.[16] These ambitions are obviously not mutually exclusive. The thought that the consumer is especially controlled by pleasure is developed much more convincingly by the sociologist Colin Campbell than by Lipovetsky.[17] Campbell describes how the traditional hedonist who gave himself up to sensual pleasures has developed into a modern, romantic hedonist who lives in and for the imaginary, ending up as the modern or postmodern consumer. Campbell emphasizes that the cultural logic of modernity is not only that of instrumental rationality but also passion and longing.[18] This is clear not least within the field of fashion. No matter what one might feel about the typical slave of fashion, it is not instrumental rationality that underlies his or her life of action. The postmodern consumer projects an idealized enjoyment onto more and more new products as the old and well-known ones gradually lose their ability to enchant. As Campbell writes, there is a connection between the ceaseless desire of the romantic for emotional stimulation and the desire of the postmodern consumer for 'the dream object' (the dream car, the dream holiday, etc.). In complete accordance with this, Richard Avedon stated in 1984 that his role as a photographer for *Vogue* consisted in 'selling dreams, not clothes'.

This romantic consumer yearns for an absolute or infinitely satisfying object but, as the Romantic Friedrich Schlegel pointed out, the one who desires the infinite does not know what he desires.[19] When he then gets the new product, it will always turn out to be a disappointment. From that point of view, the romantic and modern capitalism are perfectly suited to each other:[20] capitalism can only function as long as the consumer continues to buy new products, and the romantic consumer depends on a steady influx of new products because no product satisfies his desire. There will always be an abyss between the product as imagined and the real object. This was also a central point in Roland Barthes's study of the fashion system: the garment we desire is the garment as it is represented, but in reality we will never be able to use anything else than the 'used' garment. As Campbell expresses it, the difference between the imaginary and the real object creates a 'continuous desire' that impels consumption.[21]

The romantic emancipation from norms and restrictions gives consumption greater scope. Consumption becomes a central area for people to develop their freedom, which in turn has a consolidating effect on the consumption system.[22] Not least, consumption becomes a way of expressing one's own individuality. There are now many people who claim that the struggle against consumer society is the most important counter-cultural movement of our time. Kalle Lasn, the founder of Adbusters, claims that this movement is just as important today as, for example, feminism and environmental activism have been earlier.[23] The critique of consumer society is often based on wrong ideas about consumption, such as the idea that consumerism is synonymous with conformism – and that as a counter-culturalist one stands there as an individualist and manages in some way or other to dodge market forces. For the past forty years, however, individualism and counter-culture have been cornerstones in the advertising that seeks to make us consume more. We do not consume in order to become conformists, rather to express an individuality. If a criticism of consumption is made in the form of a criticism of conformity, one ends up in the wrong camp, because one overlooks the fact that the rhetoric of consumer society is based to an overwhelming extent on the rhetoric of classic counter-culture.

The cultural theorist Michel de Certeau and others have focused on consumption as a *meaningful* process where individuals are *creative*.[24] A main problem about the conformism interpretation is that it presents us as completely passive in relation to consumption, while we ourselves – with good reason – perceive ourselves as active and selective, and the criticism thus seems irrelevant for our self-understanding. In conformist interpretations we often get the impression that there are powerful people sitting in the fashion industry who, in dictatorial manner, decide how all of us are to look next season. But this picture does not correspond to reality. It has never been true that consumers simply allow themselves to be dictated to by the fashion industry. If we look back a century to the time of Paul Poiret, only about 10 per cent of the garments in a normal collection met with the customers' approval.[25] There are innumerable examples of the fashion industry having attempted to launch particular shades and shapes, only to discover that customers refuse to buy them. It does not help much for a united fashion press to praise a style if the broad mass of consumers does not want it – as when Christian Lacroix was praised by the press for his short puff-ball skirt of 1987. The sale of *prêt-à-porter* in the shops went disastrously wrong and Lacroix's reputation was tarnished as a result. Consumers are active and selective, and the criticism of consumerism must correspond to consumer practice and self-understanding if it is to be credible. The idea that consumers are almost hypnotized by marketing was first advanced seriously in the 1950s by the cultural critic Vance Packard,[26] but despite the fact that this idea can be said to have been thoroughly refuted, it still resurfaces at regular intervals.[27] Obviously advertising has an influence, otherwise it would hardly have existed, but, rather than being 'brainwashed', consumers act deliberately.

There are otherwise hardly any limits to the degree of helplessness and confusion ascribed to the consumer in the postmodern world. Even our ability to orientate ourselves spatially apparently breaks down in the consumer society.

According to the literary theorist Frederic Jameson, 'postmodern hyperspace has finally succeeded in transcending the capacities of the individual human body to locate itself'.[28] Postmodern space, created in the late capitalist phase, has apparently developed more rapidly than human subjectivity, so we have become completely disorientated. The argument is taken further by the social researcher Rob Shields, who claims that this loss of orientation has taken all control from us and we drift around more or less passively in the shopping centre.[29] Surveys of people's ability to orientate themselves and their consumer behaviour, where more traditional shopping centres have been compared with more 'postmodern' ones, indicate that people do not seem to have much trouble finding their bearings.[30] Even the buildings that are most complex in terms of architecture did not lead to people being overwhelmed or pacified. They tended rather to try and find their bearings – and did so quite quickly. Nor did they seem to be stimulated to consume more than usual, shopping in accordance with their usual preferences. Postmodern consumer society *is* over-complex, and commodities *have* acquired a lot of power, but it is unnecessary to exaggerate these features as extremely as some theorists do.

A more considered and plausible critique is to be found in Georg Simmel's *The Philosophy of Money* (1900), where he describes how everything in culture becomes objectivized, how the fetish nature that Marx ascribed to the commodity applies to every cultural phenomenon, and the alienation that Marx described in the relation between worker and product applies generally to modern man's relation to his surroundings.[31] For Simmel, consumption is a privileged field for the cultivation of the self, because the self is formed in an interaction with objects – including other subjects as well – in the world, and consumption offers rich opportunities for such interaction. Consumption requires an integration between consumer and the object of consumption. The greater the symbolic distance between the self and the object, the more demanding the integration task becomes. The separation between worker and product that Marx thematized via the concept of 'alienation' creates precisely such a symbolic distance; when as a consumer one has to acquire the product with the aid of money, it calls for a greater symbolic effort for the object to be integrated into the self. The modern world is furthermore characterized by an enormous increase in the amount of objects the consumer can choose between. According to Simmel, the consumer is simply overwhelmed by this plethora of commodities and this leads to the consumer not managing to integrate the consumer object adequately into his life project, with the result that the subject is at the mercy of the changes in objective culture (i.e. things), rather than being able to make things into tools for his own life project:

> The development of modern culture is characterized by the preponderance of what one may call the objective spirit over the subjective spirit. This is to say, in language as well as in law, in the technique of production as well as in art, in science as well as in the objects of the domestic environment, there is embodied a sum of spirit. The individual in his intellectual development follows the growth of this spirit very imperfectly and at an ever greater distance.[32]

It could be said that the subject is declared without authority by the objects. In this context he refers specifically to the relationship between fashions in clothes and users of them.[33] Clothes ought to be adapted to the subjects, since they were originally created by subjects to be used by subjects, but instead it is the subjects that have to adapt to the objects (the clothes). The writer Giacomo Leopardi describes this in his 'Dialogue between Fashion and Death', where Fashion says:

> In fact, generally speaking, I persuade and force all civilized people to put up every day with a thousand difficulties and a thousand discomforts, and often with pain and agony, and some even to die gloriously, for the love they bear me. I don't wish to mention the headaches, the colds, inflammations of every sort, the quotidian, tertian and quartan fevers that men get in order to obey me, being willing to shiver with cold or swelter in the heat according to my wishes, covering their heads with woollen cloth and their breasts with linen, and doing everything harmful to them . . . [34]

What is created by subjects and for subjects become objects that detach themselves from their origin and begin to follow their own logic. Modern culture is an inevitable result of the development of culture, where commodities, knowledge and technology gain dominance over humanity. That is the core of what Simmel refers to as 'the tragedy of culture'.[35] As Simmel sees things, man is outmanoeuvred by an objective spirit that he himself has created. A reaction to this is that individuals attempt to emphasize themselves as something special. Individuals are 'more and more composed of impersonal content and offers that seek to supplant the genuine personal accents and characteristics – so that if life now wishes to save that of itself which is most personal, it must make a supreme effort when it comes to being distinctive and special.'[36]

The paradoxical thing is that the attempt is made by consuming objects with a particular symbolic value. We seek our identity in what surrounds us in the now, in the symbolic values that are accessible to us. In the last resort, as absolutely individualized, without anything collective to fall back on, we go after brand names in order to individualize ourselves. Paradoxically enough, we go after highly abstract and impersonal entities in order to show who we are as unique individuals. As Simmel stresses in his philosophy of fashion, fashion always contains two opposing elements, on the one hand allowing individuals to show themselves as themselves, but at the same time always showing them as members of a group. To put on a fashion item is, from this point of view, to be a walking paradox, since at the same time one embraces and expresses both individualism and conformity.

Which symbols one acquires is to say something about who one is. Bourdieu writes: 'What is at stake is indeed "personality", i.e., the quality of the person which is affirmed in the capacity to appropriate an object of quality.'[37] What is meant by 'quality' here is completely determined by the social field. It is not a question of the innate qualities of objects but of the symbolic properties ascribed to them in the social field. We need *reasons* for preferring one thing rather than another in a consumer society. We need *differences*. These differences we buy, not least in the form of symbolic values. To a great extent we can say that the symbolic value has replaced the utility value, that is, that our relationship to objects has increasingly less to do with use. Of course, objects have utility values – and generally speaking must have them. Purely 'decorative objects' are an exception, but utility value on its own is insufficient to separate products from each other. A distinction is needed, but this can be extremely marginal. It is often the case that the distinctions become more important the smaller they are. The principle of a 'marginal difference' is particularly obvious within the field of fashionwear, although it has spread to all kinds of objects. We can hardly say that a suit from Paul Smith has an essentially different or greater utility value that one from Matalan, even though it costs ten times as much. The difference is symbolic, not functional. The difference in economic value cannot be explained on the basis of a difference in utility value. And not only have all commodities been turned into symbols – all symbols have also been turned into commodities. Baudrillard is perhaps the writer who has drawn the most extreme conclusions from this. As early as 1968, he writes that if consumption has any meaning at all, it consists in the systematic manipulation of *signs*.[38] He defines consumption as the consumption of signs, claiming that an object must first be transformed into a sign if it is to become a consumption object. This could be summed up as claiming that the truth about an object is its brand name.[39]

More than ever before, the symbolic value of things is vital for our identity and social self-realization.[40] And things have also become more like advertisements than traditional commodities. What is sold is the *idea* of a product, and as a consumer one buys an affiliation to that idea. Anyone tempted to think this is a completely new way of thinking is mistaken. When the first shopping centres were established, from the mid-nineteenth century onwards, they were places where the experience of shopping was to be central, which is why there were art exhibitions and live music in the richly decorated localities. When Selfridges opened in London in 1909, it was marketed in a way that avoided the direct marketing of anything as trivial as merchandise: it was an *experience of luxury* that was emphasized. As early as 1907 an employee in the decoration department at Wanamaker's store on East 10th Street, New York, is reported as saying: 'People do not buy the thing; they buy the effect.'[41] The idea that the most important sales item is not the material object but rather a 'metaproduct' is, then, anything but new.

All commodities gain a 'cultural' component. As the situationist Guy Debord pointed out as early as 1967: once culture has become a commodity, it also becomes the actual 'star commodity'.[42] He forecast that culture would become the driving force in the economy towards the end of the twentieth century, just as the railways had been in the latter half of the nineteenth century and the motor car was in the first part of the twentieth. It is not difficult to see that this forecast was fairly accurate. It is the 'cultural' not the 'material' aspect of commodities that is for sale. According to Baudrillard, all consumption is the consumption of symbolic signs. Even the commodity is only a *sign* when it has been liberated from all functional considerations. This sign can also lose any connection with its origins. A highly eloquent example of this is the brand Jill Sander, named after the designer Jill Sander. In 1999 Jill Sander sold the share majority of the Jill Sander company to Prada. Most people forecast that it would not be a happy marriage. They were right: five months later Jill Sander left the Jill Sander company. So what did Prada do? Well, it continued to produce Jill Sander clothes, even though Jill Sander had nothing to do with them any more. The brand name has broken completely loose of its founding designer.

An important reason why the brand label gradually became so important was that it became increasingly easy, and not least increasingly less expensive, to imitate expensive clothes through the use of synthetic materials, more efficient production and other methods, etc. A cheap copy could be found on the street at practically the same moment as the expensive original was put in the display window. Such copying is not a new phenomenon. The *haute couture* collections for Worth and Poiret were not simply created with an eye to rich customers but also in order to be copied and sold in much more reasonable versions in shops – not least in the US.[43] Worth was the first man to put brand labels with his name on clothes, to distinguish the 'genuine copies' from the 'false' ones, but as early as the 1880s false brand labels were being produced.[44] Pirate copying became a major industry after that, especially in the US; this was considered a major problem for dress designers, who did their utmost to protect their brand names.[45] The practice of distinguishing between 'genuine' and 'false' copies was continued by other dress designers. It was possible, for example, to buy an 'original copy' from Dior, that is a garment sewn on the basis of 'original drawings'. These were not to be thought of as cheap copies. But what is really the difference between a 'genuine' and a 'false' garment? 'Genuine' designwear and copies are often produced in the same factories in Asia.[46] The garments are, then, identical in terms of quality, functionality and appearance. The copy is identical to the 'genuine' article in every respect except that the copy does not pay a fee to the fashion house that has designed the garment and has the rights to the brand name – and that the consumer only pays a fraction of the price for the copy. What is actually wrong about copies? Erling Dokk Holm writes: 'The false commodity is – when revealed – an attack on the very idea of products having a meaning over and above that which is purely functional, technical or aesthetic.'[47] The copy, or forgery, undermines a symbolic dimension in which considerable resources have been invested. The person who produces or wears a copy creates an inflation in the brand, and weakens investment in those who have the 'genuine' article. From that point of view, the owner of an 'original' suffers a financial loss imposed by the wearer of a copy.

That the fashion houses try to combat pirate copying is obvious, as it imposes an economic loss on them. This loss can be of two types: they lose income because the consumer does not buy the original article or because the copy weakens the value of the brand name by creating inflation in it. The brand is the actual life-blood of the fashion houses. To be able to survive they have to sell a sufficiently large quantity of this brand. A practice that increases the sale of the brand is licensing, where others buy the right to use a brand name on an object. Elsa Schiaparelli was the first fashion designer who entered into licence agreements in the 1930s, but it is a practice that has its roots in Worth and Poiret. It is difficult to say who has licensed his or her logo to most products, but Pierre Cardin can count more than 800 such agreements. Certain fashion houses, including Chanel, have had a very moderate licensing practice, but for many of the houses it has been one of their most important sources of income. In one sense such licensing is an excellent idea, as it generates a relatively large income without one having to lift a finger. On the other hand, licensing leads to a dilution of the brand and, in the long term, can make it almost valueless. After explosive growth in licensing in the 1980s and '90s the fashion houses would seem now to have adopted a more restrictive line.

A long time has passed since the fashion market focused on a small handful of extremely prosperous clients. The entire economy of the industry comes from a large group of anonymous consumers. Even though a recognition of *haute couture* is naturally important for prestige, it is the sale of *prêt-à-porter*, accessories, perfumes and licensing that guarantees income. Bags and other accessories account for 65 per cent of Gucci's turnover. Paul Poiret was the first fashion designer to launch his own perfume, 'Rosine' (1911), and today all fashion houses have a wide range of perfumes – which, of all products on this earth, is surely the one that promises the greatest difference between production costs and sales price. It is the actual perfume bottle one pays for, not the contents. Generally speaking, perfumes have been a more 'conservative' product line than clothes and there have been fewer attempts to challenge traditional norms for how a perfume should smell. An exception to the rule is Comme des Garçons' 'Odeur 53', which is an *eau de toilette* that, according to the advertisements, is meant to smell of metal, cellulose, nail polish remover, burnt rubber and other essences. It is doubtful whether anyone is actually going to use such an *eau de toilette* and it is most reasonable to consider production as an investment in the brand name, with Comme des Garçons consolidating its reputation for being avant-garde.

Until the early 1970s the actual labels were quite small and placed inside the clothes, but since then they have become increasingly visible – except on clothes targeted at real connoisseurs who do not need a label to identify a designer costume, and where the visible label is demonstratively absent. Labels became ever larger and were positioned more and more centrally on clothes and accessories. The widespread use of licensing strengthened this trend; in addition, all the unauthorized, cheap copies often went in for even larger labels. I recall how in my teens I removed the crocodile from a worn-out Lacoste shirt and sewed it onto a cheap shirt. The actual shirt from Lacoste was basically not what I had paid a fancy price for; it was more the label, which was just as fine even when the shirt was worn out. The product I had bought was the label itself – what it was attached to was of less importance.

It is difficult *not* to be brand-conscious in today's society, where even small children of five or seven, who usually have a vocabulary of between five hundred and a thousand words, can recognize some one hundred and fifty or two hundred brands. Furthermore, even those who claim that brands are not important for them allow brands to play a significant role when evaluating products. In surveys comparing consumer evaluations of two articles that are identical, except for one being a brand name and the other 'brandless', the branded commodities are judged more positively by all groups – including those that claim not to be interested in brand names. Among other things, the brand item is perceived as being of higher quality.[48] An item can even be attractive solely because it bears a high-profile brand – what type of commodity it is can be quite subordinate. In 1999 the graphic designer Fiona Jack persuaded a company in Auckland to sponsor an advertising campaign for the title *Nothing*™, with large advertising posters being set up with slogans like 'What you've been looking for' and 'Wonderful just the way you are'. When the campaign was concluded, one third of the population of Auckland knew about the brand, and a number of people phoned to find out where they could buy this product. *Nothing*™ was an attractive symbol despite the fact that no one knew what the product was – and which in reality was precisely 'nothing'.[49]

Why do we go in for symbol consumption? The commonest answer is that we want to build up an identity. Symbol consumption is something we encountered earlier, when, for example, people consumed in order to show affiliation to a class. This is what was central for such theorists as Veblen, Simmel and Bourdieu. But this perspective is less informative today because it is so strongly based on a class concept that no longer applies.[50] Today's consumption is not so much related to class identity as to *personal* identity. But it is here that the postmodern consumer is sure to fail. Veblen's consumer can succeed by displaying class affiliation via his consumption. The postmodern consumer, on the other hand, cannot establish personal identity via his consumption, because this consumption's focusing on the moment precisely undermines the formation of identity. If one's identity is directly linked to the things that surround one, or rather to the things' symbolic value, this identity will be just as transient as those symbolic values.

Moreover, what exactly these symbols symbolize is just as unclear. What do they *mean*? There have been earlier attempts to reveal a fairly specific content in such symbolic values, for example by Roland Barthes in *Mythologies*, but very few people today seem to believe that symbolic values can be said to have a specific semantic content. As shown in chapter Four on fashion and language, clothes also function badly as a means of communication. The same applies to most other commodities. Of course, a dress from Dolce&Gabbana or a suit from Issey Miyake tell other people something (that one is a fashion-conscious person who has money to spend on clothes), but that can scarcely be said to be an utterance fraught with meaning.

Today, practically every product is saturated with meaning – even the most trivial bottle of mineral water has to contain all sorts of messages – but it is also becoming increasingly clear that hardly any of this *means* anything at all. According to the sociologist Harvie Ferguson: 'The commodity can become a sign only because it has been emptied of intrinsic value. Its power to represent depends on its inner insignificance.'[51] Ferguson's formulation is exaggerated, and it is not true that an object can only gain sign value if it has been stripped of all other value, but the point is that the sign value has become increasingly central and has gradually come to overshadow all other value. The commodities come to an increasing extent with prefabricated meanings, in order to create a particular consumer response.[52] Max Horkheimer and Theodor W. Adorno make a similar assertion, linked to Kant's theory of interpretation, so-called schematism:

> Kant's formalism still expected a contribution from the individual, who was thought to relate the varied experiences of the senses to fundamental concepts; but industry robs the individual of his function. Its prime service to the customer is to do his schematizing for him. [. . .] There is nothing left for the consumer to classify. Producers have done it for him.[53]

As they see it, the product has already been fully interpreted when it meets the consumer, who simply passively takes over the prefabricated meaning. This is not completely true, however, if we look more closely at the attitude consumers adopt to the meaning of commodities. Commodities acquire meanings that exceed what the producers had placed in them. Quite often, other consumer segments than those envisaged by the producer start using the product and add new meanings to it. One example of this is when the long-established Norwegian brand Helly Hansen suddenly became fashionable in American hip-hop environments – and gained connotations far removed from its origins in Norwegian outdoor life. The media expert John Fiske goes to the opposite extreme of Horkheimer and Adorno and presents consumption culture as a 'semiotic democracy', where consumers actively reinterpret the symbols for their own purposes. According to Fiske, shopping is actually a meaning-laden political activity, and he talks about young consumers as 'shopping mall guerrillas par excellence'.[54] This is obviously an exaggeration. Most products do not have *essentially* different meanings ascribed to them than those the producer has placed in them, even though this occurs in some cases; even when it does occur, this does not mean that they play some important political role. Most of those who shop are not particularly motivated by the political aspects of the activity. The meaning of the items is socially determined: it could be said that their meaning is the subject of 'negotiations' between various parties, where no party can decide completely that a given product has one particular meaning. The transformation of the product's 'meaning' that is perhaps most widespread is that the meaning evaporates relatively quickly once it has reached the market.

We see this particularly clearly in connection with the appropriation by the market of subcultural phenomena.[55] The cultural theorist Dick Hebdige presents subcultures as cultures of conspicuous consumption.[56] Subcultural styles have on the whole a greater semantic content than the mass-cultural ones, and this meaning will often not be accessible to outsiders. To an outsider the subculture may seem to lack any form of order, but in actual fact even the most 'anarchistic' subculture, such as punk, is extremely well-ordered.[57] Subcultures normally cultivate individuality, but in that respect they are completely in accordance with mass-culture. New subcultures create new fashions and trends that are taken up by industry. Subcultures or counter-cultures have become the best friend of fashion and capital.[58] As the cultural critic Thomas Frank has put it:

> The counter-cultural idea has become capitalist orthodoxy, its lust for transgression on transgression

> now perfectly adapted to an economic-cultural regime that runs on ever-faster cyclings of the new; its taste for self-fulfilment and its intolerance for the confines of tradition now permitting vast latitude in consuming practices and lifestyle experimentation.[59]

A counter-culture produces differences in order to be able to define itself as an opposition to the existing culture, but the consumption that furthers capital has precisely to do with such differences, ones that capital can incorporate into its own logic.[60] In Don DeLillo's novel *Cosmopolis* major demonstrations against global capitalism take place, and inside a large white limousine surrounded by demonstrators sits the main character of the book, a young billionaire, who remarks:

> This is the free market itself. These people are a fantasy generated by the market. They don't exist outside the market. There is nowhere they can go to be on the outside. There is no outside . . . The market culture is total. It breeds these men and women. They are necessary to the system they despise. They give it energy and definition. They are market-driven. They are traded on the markets of the world. This is why they exist, to invigorate and perpetuate the system.[61]

Hebdige claims that punk clothing is equivalent to swearing.[62] But precisely because it was 'shocking', this style was an obvious candidate for being incorporated into fashion (even if in a diluted version), since that is exactly the kind of effect fashion has been dependent on for many decades in its attempt to seem innovative. This process, however, leads to the subcultural style rapidly being emptied of meaning. As early as 1977 – the year when punk 'officially' came into being, although the previous year would have been a more accurate date – punk became domesticated and made harmless via articles in newspapers and magazines, where the focus was on how 'cool' punk rockers' clothes were.[63] This meant in practice that they had already been assimilated by mass fashion. From the fashion perspective, there is no real opposition between a counter-culture and what already exists. Everything can be incorporated, as when the former junkie William S. Burroughs appeared in Nike advertisements, and Gap used pictures by Jack Kerouac in ads for trousers. All the world's rebels will, if their revolt manages to reach beyond a limited environment, end up seeing their style reproduced in exquisite materials and at high prices. If we look at how advertisements are designed, until the early 1960s they had to a great extent to do with 'conforming', since when they have dealt to an increasing extent with *not* conforming, with being a 'rebel' and an 'individualist'. The slogan in an advertisement for Hugo Boss urges: 'Don't imitate, Innovate!' What is innovative, apparently, is to buy goods from Boss. But how innovative is that, really?

We seek identity and shop symbolic values, knowing full well that they never last. To counteract this lack of durability we are constantly searching for something new. We become major consumers of new things, new places and new people. The focus on symbolic value leads to the rate of turnover increasing all the time because it is controlled by the logic of fashion. The inherent value and functionality of things then become less important, and their lifespan is at the mercy of changes in fashion. The nature of fashion is to produce effective signs that shortly afterwards become ineffective signs. The principle of fashion is to create a constantly increasing velocity, to make an object become superfluous as quickly as possible so as to move on to a new one. It could almost be said that the point of operating a postmodern business is not to satisfy the needs consumers have but rather of creating new needs. We want new needs because the old ones bore us. We are hooked on experiences, and experiences are all about emotional stimulus. Market analyses cannot tell companies what these needs are, because they do not yet exist. So there is no alternative but to invent new needs, new stimuli.

As we saw in chapter Three, Simmel claims that the greater the extent to which we are exposed to the rapid changes of fashion, the greater the need will be for cheap versions of the commodity – something which in turn increases the speed of the fashion changes. The awareness of the power of fashion is an awareness that no commodities will last, and that if one is to choose a commodity that is inevitably going to change, one will tend to choose the latest fashion rather than an earlier one. Commodities do not last, nor are they meant to. Considered as purely functional objects they last, of course, and are meant to – for otherwise they would not be 'quality articles'. But their symbolic value is worn out ever more rapidly. Producers no longer have to conceal that another 'new, improved version' will soon be on its way. Indeed, this is an important part of the attraction of the postmodern item – we will soon be able to replace it![64]

Is this irrational? Of course it is! The consumer society presupposes irrational individuals, that is to say that the rationality of this society can only function if its members are irrational.[65] And we are. We consume at an ever-increasing tempo, despite the fact that deep down we know that it does not help us attain our goal. Let us look a little more closely at what this irrationality consists of. A usual element in the account of rational players is that they act with the intention of their acts having consequences that go beyond the moment of acting. A rational player must, then, possess a certain amount of far-sightedness. What is typical of the postmodern consumer is rather a constant pursuit of satisfaction in the actual moment. The time perspective is cut down almost to the moment. These perspectives are becoming shorter and shorter. This applies not only to our attitude to consumption of goods but also to other human beings. Instead of 'till death us do part', it is 'till boredom us do part' that applies. Naturally, family and friends play a decisive role in the constitution of our identities. Love and friendship are not normally things we refer to in terms of 'consumption'; the problem is that to a growing extent they are becoming subject to a model of consumption.

Michel de Montaigne has written that, of all the pleasures we know, the *pursuit* of pleasure is the greatest.[66] That sums up the modern – or perhaps, rather, the postmodern – consumer very aptly. We can understand this consumer's wish in two ways: (1) he deludes himself into believing that one day he will find something that finally can satisfy his desire, so that the pursuit can come to an end, or (2) he has realized that there is nothing that can truly satisfy his desire and he therefore retains the pursuit itself as his main interest. It is not obvious which of the two is the correct answer. Nor is there any reason to believe that all typically postmodern consumers have thought about this problem at all. But can we really assume that the postmodern consumer does not understand that he will not find a solution in any single product or amount of products? I don't think so. The postmodern consumer can seem to want satisfaction, but by his behaviour he shows that what he really wants is the *pursuit* of satisfaction, because this pursuit gives him the greatest possible satisfaction.

It is here that this consumer differs from earlier consumers. The postmodern consumer is a further development of the classic consumer. We are dealing with a historical development that stretches over several centuries and within which it is difficult to point to any clear break. So when we talk about two distinct types of consumer, it is an idealization. One can ask oneself if this consumer can ever exist in a 'pure' form at all. A feature often emphasized about the 'postmodern' consumer is that he acts out a number of conflicting identities that are expressed via the use of different styles, symbols and the like. A survey among American college students indicated that they did not have ambitions to express such opposing identities and that they rather wished to create cohesive identities by the way they dressed, preferably by looking for specific symbol values. In other words, they were more 'modern' than 'postmodern' in that respect.[67] Rather than there being a series of people who correspond completely to the image of the postmodern consumer, this player is an idealized entity, based on characteristics that are becoming increasingly common but that hardly exist in a pure form in any one person. There is, of course, much consumption that is not of this postmodern type: when I buy milk and bread, the symbolic construction of my identity does not have high priority, – but not necessarily if I choose organic milk and bread. Idealizations bring out the main point, which is that the postmodern consumer differs in nature from the classic one. For he operates according to a different logic.

The decisive feature of the consumer society is not that consumption takes place, not that it increases – even if it does so at an extreme rate. The decisive thing is that consumption to a high degree has been disconnected from what we can reasonably call the satisfaction of needs. The classic consumer had to consume, just as every other living being has to, in order to survive, and his needs could even become quite sophisticated: human life has always demanded more than the satisfaction of purely biological needs because man is also a social being, which means that needs were adjusted in accordance with *social* standards that transcended the biological ones. These standards have consequently increased. But the important thing about the classic consumer is that his consumption had a roof. This roof changed through history, in accordance with the sociomaterial development of society – but a roof was always there. And there was a floor, too. There were social norms that determined what was too little (where it was a question of poverty) or too much (where it was a question of gluttony). And this social norm was never allowed to be too far removed from the satisfaction of biological needs.[68] Consumption was clearly subject to a moral norm. These moral, social norms are no longer operative to the same extent.[69]

Now the distinction between 'natural' and 'artificial' needs is anything but easy to draw. It is easier to argue that the division between human needs that are constant and 'natural' and those that are historically changeable must of necessity remain an abstraction that will never be able to be implemented in a concrete way. As Adorno writes: 'What a person needs to live and what he does not need does not at all depend on nature but adapts itself to "the cultural minimum subsistence level". Any attempt to separate off pure nature is leading one astray.'[70] Baudrillard even goes one step further and denaturalizes needs completely by considering them to be entirely the products of the consumer society.[71] A need is considered as a need for a difference, for a social entity, and never for an object 'in itself'.[72] It is clear that Baudrillard, deliberately, is exaggerating here. Even if we are unable to draw an absolute line between 'natural' and 'artificial' needs, this does not mean that we therefore have to abandon the distinction completely. We can draw a tentative line by providing an example: even if a person has a 'natural' need for clothes in order to keep out the cold, an absolute need for the cold to be kept out by knitwear from Sonia Rykiel would be an 'artificial' need. But the point is nevertheless that the idea of 'natural needs' can no longer be normative for consumption. Consumption is no longer driven by needs but by desire. Zygmunt Bauman writes, 'The *spiritus movens* of consumer activity is not a set of articulated, let alone fixed, needs, but *desire*'.[73] When consumption aims at satisfying given needs, it has limits. When it is disconnected, it is in principle limitless.[74] We could perhaps even say that the desires have been turned into needs.

Putting this another way, for the classic consumer consumption is a means, while for the postmodern consumer it is an end in itself. But this would also be slightly misleading. When one talks about something being an end in itself, one normally talks about something that gives a satisfaction in itself, not by virtue of leading to something else. This is the role Aristotle ascribes to happiness.[75] Aristotle's main work on ethics, *Nicomachean Ethics*, begins with an investigation of what the good is. When he asks what the good is, he replies with the commonly accepted idea that it is happiness. *Happiness is an end in itself.* When we search for something, we can either search for it for its own sake or for something else's sake. The goal of medicine is health, the goal of cookery is a tasty meal, and so on. Why do the various activities search for their goals? Are good food and health ends in themselves, or are they subject to another goal – a purpose that provides the reason why all the other goals are worth searching for? Aristotle claims that the only thing we are searching for for its own sake is happiness, and that everything else is only sought to the extent that it contributes to realizing happiness. Samuel Beckett, by the way, makes a savage comment on this in the second act of his play *Waiting for Godot*, where the two tramps Vladimir and Estragon are talking together and Estragon says: 'We are happy. What do we do now, now that we are happy?' I do not know what Aristotle would have replied to Beckett, but he would probably have claimed that Beckett has not understood what happiness is, for, since happiness is the reason for everything else being sought, one cannot search for anything else when one is happy. It is rather as if two saints had arrived in heaven, looked at each other and said: 'Now we're in heaven. What do we do now?' It is perhaps not a particularly meaningful question. We see the absurdity of these questions. And yet we do not see anything absurd in asking: 'We consume and consume. What do we do now?' For that is actually a question we *must* ask ourselves. It also makes it clear that consumption is only apparently an end in itself. It pretends to be such an end in itself but it is dysfunctional. Why is it dysfunctional? We do not become happy.[76]

Consumption does not give us the meaning we are looking for – it is an *ersatz* meaning, nothing more nor less. But it is this that the modern project has been directed towards: that all of us should become full-time consumers – and that this would make us happy. It was this type of society we wanted: we have got the consumer society we have striven for. All societies have a dream of a state without lack, as in the idea of a golden age in antiquity, or of paradise in Christianity. In modern Western man it is the idea of limitless consumption that has fulfilled such a role. Consumption fills the existential vacuum where a lack could have been. Our utopia has been the consumer society – a society where we as individuals can realize ourselves via the consumption of goods.[77] According to Mr Dumby in the second act of Oscar Wilde's *Lady Windermere's Fan*, 'In this world there are only two tragedies. One is not getting what one wants, and the other is getting it. The last is much the worst; the last is a real tragedy!' So it may be a consolation that we will never get what we want if consumption is to be our goal in life, since standards are constantly changing as their fulfilment draws near. The finishing line never gets any closer.[78]

8

Fashion as an Ideal in Life

I feel like shit but look great.
Bret Easton Ellis[1]

The apparel oft proclaims the man.
Shakespeare[2]

Those who make their dress a principal part of themselves, will, in general, become of no more value than their dress.
William Hazlitt[3]

Know, first, who you are; and then adorn yourself accordingly.
Epictetus[4]

'Identity' is one of the seminal concepts for describing the function of fashion. Fashion allegedly contributes to the formation of identity. Our identities have become problematic – they are no longer something we take for granted. This is linked to a general focusing on self-realization. Self-realization is an extremely modern phenomenon. If, for example, you had asked a person from the medieval period if he was preoccupied with self-realization, he or she would not understand what you meant. It is a thought that would have been completely alien. While the pre-modern world was conceived as a static order that consisted most fundamentally of unchangeable essences, the modern world is constantly changing. It also has every source of change in itself – it is not controlled by an outside force (God). And the role of modern man in this world does not consist in realizing a given essence but in realizing himself by creating himself.

The present-day pursuit of self-realization is perhaps the absolutely clearest expression of what a grip individualism (the individual as an ideology) has got on us. Individualism is so all-pervasive that it is hard to think of anything more conformist. A couple of centuries ago, we gradually began to think of ourselves as *individuals*, this being the time when individualism started to appear on the scene.[5] The realization dawned that all individuals are different – unique, in fact. For us, the perception of ourselves as 'individuals' is so 'natural' that we find it difficult to imagine that it could have been any different, but the 'individual' is a social construction that has arisen and, in principle, can disappear again, even though it is hard for us today to see alternatives to such a self-understanding.[6] A particular feature of individuals is that they must *realize* themselves as individuals. They are put in the world with the task of having to become themselves, of realizing their unique characteristics. There is no longer one collective meaning of life in the modern world, a meaning that it is up to the individual to take part in – and that will automatically give the individual identity through participation in the collective. Instead, all of us are referred to our individual self-realization projects. *Everyone* is preoccupied with self-realization, but very few people seem to reflect much on what *kind* of self ought to be realized. Instead, it is self-realization as such that is centre stage. This self-realization would appear to be an obligation. The emergence of individualism meant a cultural emancipation of the individual, but also that the individual gained new responsibility for himself and *to become himself*.

Traditions provide constancy, but they are increasingly disintegrating as a result of the modernization process.

Lacking traditions, we are hyperactive lifestyle constructors, in an attempt to form meaning and identity. The dissolution of social classes paved the way for the emergence of lifestyles, which in turn contributed to further dissolution of classes as a result of increased differentiation. In postmodern society one's identity is determined less by financial status than before, or, more precisely, financial status has been reduced to one factor among many. For that reason, even those best off are subject to the same type of 'identity work' as everyone else, even though they undeniably have a head start in a world where identity is more and more becoming something one can buy. It is more demanding to maintain a lifestyle than membership of a social class: it calls for sustained activity. Furthermore, lifestyles go out of fashion, so that constant assessments have to be made as to what extent they ought to be retained or a new one chosen if one is to keep abreast of fashion. Pre-modern man had a more stable identity because it was anchored in a tradition, but today we have been largely liberated from the shackles of tradition, and personal identity has thus become a question of maintaining a lifestyle.[7] While a tradition is handed down, a lifestyle is chosen. The choice of one lifestyle rather than another is only loosely binding and can always be revised. If one is totally part of a tradition, one will not question it nor look for alternatives. The 'reflexive self', on the other hand, cannot avoid a chronic search for alternatives between which there are choices.

The hypothesis of the reflexive self is particularly linked to Anthony Giddens, even though it was doubtlessly anticipated by such philosophers as Fichte and Hegel. According to Giddens, a reflexive monitoring of one's behaviour is an inherent part of the self for members of every human society, both the traditional and the post-traditional.[8] In his opinion, however, modern societies are characterized by a special type of self-reflexivity, where it becomes radicalized precisely because individuals have virtually been liberated from the shackles of tradition: 'In the post-traditional order of modernity, and against the backdrop of new forms of mediated experience, self-identity becomes a reflexively organised endeavour.'[9] He also formulates it as follows: 'Fundamental features of a society of high reflexivity are the "open" character of self-identity and the reflexive nature of the body.'[10] This means that individuals increasingly have to construct a self-identity using the means that the individual has at his disposal, rather than the self appearing to be something given. The self becomes something that has to be created, monitored, maintained and changed.

This hypothesis of self-reflexivity would seem to collide with Bourdieu's theory of action, where the concept 'habitus' is central. Bourdieu's theory suggests that identity is far less workable via reflexive intervention than Giddens's theory would suggest. One's habitus is formed by social structures, and habitus generates actions that in turn reproduce the social structures. It is important to emphasize that habitus is not strictly determinative, in the sense that every action must be directly followed by habitus.[11] It is most closely related to Aristotle's concept of *hexis*, that is a basic attitude or disposition.[12] A player who functions well in a particular field will not stick slavishly to the rules of that field but, on the contrary, display a degree of flexibility. Habitus is a kind of second nature, and is basically pre-reflexive.[13] It operates at a deeper level than human consciousness: 'the schemes of the habitus, the primary forms of classification, owe their specific efficacy to the fact that they function below the level of consciousness and language, beyond the reach of introspective scrutiny or control by the will.'[14] Precisely because habitus lies deeper than consciousness, it cannot be modified as a point of departure via a conscious act of will.[15] As Bourdieu understands habitus, it cannot be the object of the type of reflexive intervention that, according to Giddens, is a basic characteristic of modern man.

If one does not wish to choose here between Giddens and Bourdieu, as both theories have attractive features, an attempt can be made to reconcile them by claiming that reflexivity has become a part of habitus. The sociologist Paul Sweetman has introduced the concept 'reflexive habitus', claiming that this is becoming increasingly common as a result of diverse economic, social and cultural changes.[16] He refers in particular to changes in work, social relations and a consumer culture that challenge us constantly to monitor and 'improve' ourselves. Bourdieu also opens up the possibility of reflexivity, claiming that it will only develop if some crisis or other occurs that leads to the field and habitus not matching each other. If the fields within which the players operate are subject to many rapid changes, such a non-match ought precisely to occur, resulting in reflexivity becoming a more or less permanent state.

Even though reflexivity should have become a permanent state and thus made habitus considerably more flexible, Bourdieu's theory nevertheless contains an important corrective to the hypothesis of the reflexive self. The hypothesis can create an impression of the self as something almost sovereignly self-propulsive, thereby concealing how exposed this self is to forces outside itself and what limitations the forming of the own self will always be subject to. We can say with Bourdieu that habitus always limits the potential space for action. The aestheticization of life is not accessible to everyone, also for economic reasons.[17] Admittedly, the boundaries have not been laid down once and for all. They can change, but they cannot change completely as the individual player sees fit. Self-identity is not constituted by a self-sufficient self but always created on the basis of social relations.

Even if we now recognize that there are socio-material limitations on the choice of lifestyle, we are nevertheless obliged to make a choice. We must choose a lifestyle and, as a style, the choice is basically an *aesthetic* one. Aesthetics, then,

142 becomes a centre for the formation of identity. The question is to what extent this is a particularly promising strategy. Fashion is of course central to this ideology of aesthetic self-realization. Fashion has functioned as an arena where we could find ourselves or, more precisely, invent ourselves. The fashion industry took upon itself the mission of saving us from the hard work of having to create ourselves as a work of art by enabling us instead to buy a readymade package from a fashion house. As Renzo Rosso of Diesel Jeans has said: 'We don't sell a product, we sell a style of life . . . The Diesel concept is everything.'[18] Similarly, Oscar de la Renta says: 'In the old days fashion designers – seamstresses really – made and sold only dresses; today we sell a lifestyle to the whole world.'[19] Pierre Cardin was a pioneer of this way of thinking, attempting to create a whole world one could live in. He not only created clothes but also interior design, leisure items and even a chain of restaurants, so that it was possible to let one's entire existence be permeated by one style.

It must be emphasized, however, that a person will not be completely fashionable if he or she follows fashion *too* well. A hint of personal taste should also be suggested, for example by combining two garments in a distinctive way. Fashion is always to be found in the interspace between the individual and the conformist. To count as a fashion, both conformity and individuality must be taken into consideration. Individuality is only meaningful against a background of a heavy conformity. If you want to appear individual, you must do so against a backdrop of conformity. Fashion is always a compromise between these two, as Simmel pointed out long ago. If there is too much individuality, it loses its appeal, because then it no longer functions distinctively, and then as fashion it is dead. In an age like ours, where norms have broadened considerably and many norms run parallel, it is more difficult to mark individuality precisely because there is now so much room for major variations.

Plurality in the field of fashion is not least a product of the enormous amount of visual information that bombards us every day. Susan Sontag claims that a society becomes modern when one of its main activities is to produce and consume images.[20] In that case, we are close to living in the most modern of all possible worlds. All of us have become 'image junkies', as Sontag puts it.[21] According to Hal Foster, we are unable to escape the logic of the image, because images both create a loss of reality and at the same time give us something – namely new images – that enable us to soften or deny this loss.[22] The image becomes a substitute for reality. Hannah Arendt writes: 'The reality and reliability of the world rest primarily on the fact that we are surrounded by things more permanent than the activity by which they were produced, and potentially even more permanent than the lives of their authors.'[23] Conversely, a world where the lifespan of things is completely at the mercy of the whims of fashion is an unreal and unreliable world. For Lipovetsky, fashion becomes the life-guide, because it trains us to live in a world where everything is constantly changing.[24] Viewed this way, fashion ought to be an ideal life-guide for a world whose premises it has set itself. The question is whether it really can fulfil such a role.

There is little in Nietzsche's writings about fashion, but he frames a conception of man that in certain respects is highly suited to fashion. The supreme commandment is: 'You shall become the person you are.'[25] This is not least a question of 'adding style' to one's nature.[26] He claims: 'Only as an aesthetic phenomenon is existence still endurable for us.'[27] This thought is taken further in Michel Foucault's late philosophy. Foucault claims that the present task for each and every one of us is to create ourselves as works of art.[28] He disassociates himself from every conception of humanity that ascribes to it a given essence that must be sought for. The task is not to *find* oneself but to *invent* oneself. Foucault sees the individual as a social construction. In his earlier work, Foucault stressed how individuals are formed by power relations, especially by such social institutions as the health and prison services.[29] In writings in the years immediately before his death in 1984, this perspective changed considerably: he still considers the subject as a construction, but widens this conception by now claiming that it is a construction that also possesses the ability to construct itself. This self-construction takes place, among other things, by means of what Foucault calls 'asceticism', which means that the subject carries out ongoing work on himself in order to become his own master.[30] But this conception of being one's own master can seem paradoxical, since it is a question of being a master of a self that is constantly moving away from itself. Foucault claims that his whole work has been an attempt to liberate himself from himself, to prevent himself from remaining the same person.[31] What is this self striving for? How does this self organize its life? Foucault does not come all that much nearer an account of this as an ideal than to emphasize lifestyle as an attractive concept for the formation of the self, since a lifestyle can contain both an ethical and an aesthetic aspect.[32] But a lifestyle can be so many things.

Foucault also links to Baudelaire's fascination with the dandy, who is seen as some sort of ideal.[33] Is this dandy an ideal worth striving for? The dandy is a figure that emerged in England at the turn of the nineteenth century. After the French Revolution it was not so much the style of the aristocrat as of the gentleman that was in accordance with the values of the time. The dandy wore clothes of relatively simple design, the vital thing being that they were made of the best materials and a cut that bore witness to a sophisticated, individual taste. Carlyle gives a good contemporary description of the dandy:

> A Dandy is a Clothes-wearing Man, a Man whose trade, office, and existence consists in the wearing of Clothes. Every faculty of his soul, spirit, purse, and person is heroically consecrated to this one object, the

> wearing of clothes wisely and well: so that as others dress to live, he lives to dress.[34]

Another dandy, Oscar Wilde, claimed that 'one should either be a work of art or wear a work of art.'[35] The dandy spent hours in front of the mirror, with a concentration on detail that bordered on the ludicrous. But all the effort put into presenting a perfect exterior was not to be visible. The dandy above all dandies, Beau Brummell, said: 'If John Bull turns round to look after you, you are not well dressed; but either too stiff, too tight, or too fashionable.'[36] Sobriety became an ideal for beauty, characterized by perfectionism rather than ostentatious luxury. The dandy strove for a self-evident and relaxed impression, even though a great deal of work lay behind his perfect exterior. As Baudelaire emphasizes: 'The dandy is blasé, or pretends to be so, for reasons of policy and caste.'[37] For that reason, a snob will never be a successful dandy – the snob displays all too clearly that he is a status-seeker. A contemporary of Beau Brummell describes how Brummell was the ruler of a whole generation of people with the cut of his clothes.[38] The style of the dandy was actually crucial for the development of middle-class fashion, with its focus on the discreet, without exaggerated features. Once the middle class had taken over the dandy's style, this became more explicitly extravagant and affected towards the end of the nineteenth century. An example of this type of dandy was Comte Robert de Montesquieu, who was the model for Des Esseintes, the main character of Joris-Karl Huysmans' novel *À rebours* (1884). He wore white suits with a small bouquet of violets at his throat instead of a tie. It is this image that has led to the later understanding of a dandy as someone who is outré and a slightly fatuous figure – an ideal that Beau Brummell would hardly have met with anything but scorn.

What is it about the dandy that we ought to see as exemplary? Is he an ideal for us? Here it can be worth listening to a 'repentant' dandy. While the young Oscar Wilde cultivated a non-committal play with surfaces, the older Wilde often repeats: 'The supreme vice is shallowness.'[39] The dandy remains on the surface. He never becomes anything other than a changing stream of masks, and therefore never becomes himself. 'A man whose desire is to be something separate from himself . . . invariably succeeds in being what he wants to be. That is his punishment. Those who want a mask have to wear it.'[40] Wilde does not at all renounce the individualism he has always advocated in his writing, but totally changes the understanding of how it must be formed. He states an individualistic imperative that he feels most people do not live up to.[41] To live according to categories set up by others is to become those others and not oneself. How is one to become oneself? It is not a question of uncovering an underlying, given 'true' self but of *being* oneself. In order to be oneself, however, one must maintain a link with one's past and future. Because the dandy only becomes a stream of changing masks, he denies his former self and thus denies himself.[42] To establish a self calls for maintaining a connection: who one has been and who one is to become.

According to the philosopher Charles Taylor:

> There are questions about how I am going to live my life which touch on the issue of what life is worth living, or what kind of life would fulfil the promise implicit in my particular talents, or the demands incumbent on someone with my endowment, or of what constitutes a rich, meaningful life – as against one concerned with secondary matters or trivia. These are issues of strong evaluation, because the people who ask these questions have no doubt that one can, following one's immediate wishes and desires, take a wrong turn and hence fail to lead a full life.[43]

The central concept here is 'strong evaluations'. These are normative evaluations that deal with what sort of person one wishes to be. Weak evaluations deal with the results of actions, whether they give a pleasant result or the like, whereas strong evaluations have to do with one's nature. For Taylor, identity is inextricably linked to ethics, to personal questions of what sort of life one should realize. These questions are asked and answered within a historical and social context. Our values are initially given to us by the society in which we grow up and these constitute our identity to a considerable extent. Here, however, a problem arises for modern Western man. That which characterizes modern societies is that they are fragmentary. They are no longer characterized by a self-evident set of values that the individual internalizes. Pre-modern societies have a given framework of values that set a standard against which one can measure one's life, but frameworks for the strong evaluations have become problematic in the modern world.[44] Therefore, our identities are no longer given us as something that is self-evident. Taylor claims therefore that values, and consequently identities, are to a greater extent something that have to be *chosen* by each individual. Seen in this way, identity becomes something that must be created, and this creation takes place on the basis of an interpretation of who one is and a strong evaluation of who one should be. But on the basis of what standards is such an evaluation to be undertaken when the frameworks have become so problematic? We ought at any rate to attempt to carry them out on the basis of an understanding of what it means to have a self that can live a fully worthy life.

Taylor also writes that one way these existential questions present themselves to us has to do with:

> whether our lives have unity, or whether one day is just following the next without purpose or sense, the past falling into a kind of nothingness which is not the

> prelude, or harbinger, or opening, or early stage of anything, whether it is just 'temps perdu' in the double sense intended in the title of Proust's celebrated work, that is time which is both wasted and irretrievably lost, beyond recall, in which we pass as if we had never been.[45]

This is an apt comment on the self that has fashion as its model. According to Lipovetsky, fashion has created a new type of person, 'the fashion person', who does not connect strongly to anything or anyone, and who has a constantly changing personality and taste.[46] What remains of this person when we remove the clothes of fashion? The fashion expert Holly Brubach says that she keeps old clothes in her wardrobe even though she never intends to wear them again 'out of respect for those people I used to be. They meant well. Each one gave way to the next and disappeared, leaving only her clothes behind.'[47] Madonna is depicted by many people as a prize example of a late or postmodern subject, constantly reinventing herself via radically new styles.[48] Fashion is allegedly the missing essence of the postmodern self, which is programmed constantly to go off in search of new versions of itself, but it becomes a self without any constancy whatsoever – a self that disappears without ever having been itself.

The philosopher Paul Ricoeur distinguishes between two aspects of the self, which we can refer to respectively as *sameness* and *selfness*.[49] Sameness has to do with remaining the same person, even though one is in a process of change. Even though a person changes a good deal in the course of a life, we believe that it is the *same* person who has undergone these changes. A second aspect of the self is what Ricoeur calls selfness, which has to do with self-identity, that the person is a reflexive being that relates to himself or herself. He insists on both aspects, both sameness and selfness, being necessary in order to have a self. But how are sameness and selfness connected to each other? They must be placed in a context, and this context consists in one telling a cohesive story of who one has been and who one is to become. In this narrative, past, present and future are gathered into a unity, and through this a unity of the self is also created. To be a self is to be able to give an account of a self through a narrative of who one has been, who one will become and who one is now. To tell this narrative of oneself is to *become* oneself. Here we can see what the problem is with the 'fashion self'. It is a hyper-reflexive self, thus fulfilling the demand of selfness, but since it is only a stream of new, soon to be discarded figures that disappear without trace and without being related to each other, its selfness is undermined. It is a self without a cohesive narrative.[50] The fashion self is not only a self without a real past, because this past is always forgotten in favour of a present, it is also a self without a future, simce this future is completely random. Fashion does not have any final goal – it is not going anywhere except forwards.

Self-identity is not at all some given, unchangeable entity. It has to be told and retold, and it changes each time it is retold. This applies to both modern and pre-modern societies, but a central trait about modernity is that individuals to an increasing extent have to create their *own* narratives about themselves, since the collective narratives no longer have so much buoyancy. A construction of identity never starts completely from scratch, but is having increasingly to do so because the social instances that have traditionally helped to create a constancy of the self have become considerably looser and less stable.

A human life needs some kind of unity, but it is precisely that unity which cannot be established using fashion as a model. Søren Kierkegaard's critique of the aesthetic way of life in *Either/Or* is still relevant today.[51] Kierkegaard emphasizes that the aesthete is characterized by immediacy, not in the sense of openness but in the sense of dependency on everything he has round about him. The aesthete lives in a state of despair. There are two reasons for the aesthete despairing. The first is connected to the fact that there is something random and transient about his life: the exterior can collapse at any moment. Clearly the aesthete's life can be successful, provided the outer conditions are maintained, but they can always let him down – his life is built on sand. The second reason is that man is a spiritual being, something the aesthete more or less denies, and it is precisely this denial that creates melancholy. The aesthete is half aware that he is denying his real self. He is in need of a view of life that can provide him with something firm and unchanging in the constant flux of life. The aesthete lacks 'continuity' and lives without any recollection of his own life.[52] This leads to his life dissolving into empty noise devoid of content.[53] So a change is necessary, one that can only take place via a leap into a new form of life – the ethical stage – which can establish the cohesion lacking in the aesthetic stage. The ethicist chooses himself, and via that choice does not necessarily change his outer life, but a fixed point is established for his inner life. In the way he conducts his outer life the ethicist may remain unchanged – the change has to do with the relationship the ethicist has to outer things and to himself. If we say that the aesthete is a person who has fashion as an ideal in life, then the ethicist does not have to renounce fashion. The important difference is that the ethicist will not base his identity on fashion but have an independence in relation to it.

Fashion can give us tools to shape a social identity that is not primarily concerned with class or status, but it is not a particularly solid tool. A further problem in this connection is the apparently unlimited plurality (or perhaps pluralism is the better word) in present-day fashion. As shown in chapter Two, fashion was formerly driven forward by a logic of replacement, where a new fashion sought to make all previous fashions superfluous by turning them into a thing of the past, something that had gone out of fashion. Now the prevailing tendency is to supplement rather than to replace. This marks a radical change, one that can be said to mean a total break with the essence of fashion itself. As a consequence of fashion's lack of any restrictions there is reason to believe that its potential to change identity will become less and less. Even so, this potential is not completely insignificant. We cannot avoid giving others an impression of who we are by what we wear. And it is also crucial for our perception of ourselves and our position in the world. Virginia Woolf points out in *Orlando* that clothes have far more important tasks than to keep us warm: 'They change our view of the world and the world's view of us.'[54] In an apt formulation she writes that it is clothes that wear us and not we them. In *Down and Out in Paris and London*, George Orwell talks of how he suddenly found himself in a different world when he dressed as a tramp and how everyone suddenly began to treat him completely differently.[55] Clothes are objects that create behaviour by expressing social identity. It is not that one first has an identity and then chooses to express it via certain clothes, or that there is an 'inner' identity independent of all outer representations that can subsequently be given expression by various means, including clothes. The argument could just as easily be reversed and the claim be made that it is the outer that constitutes the inner, that it is clothes that constitute identity. But that would also be misleading. It is impossible to give absolute priority to either the internal or the external aspect of identity: they are mutually dependent on each other.

To try to oppose fashion, for example by using one type of apparel (perhaps a black suit and black shirt) exclusively for every occasion, is also just a question of playing a role. It is no more 'authentic' to walk around in an ankle-length coat every day, proclaiming 'I am an artist who despises present-day fashions', than to only appear in suits by Paul Smith, and it certainly does not imply that one should necessarily have more of a 'core' to one's identity. Simmel does not consider the person who tries to escape from fashion as an ideal, but nor does he believe that such a person is fleeing from the modern life of which he or she is actually a part. Seen in such a way, fleeing from fashion would simply be escapism. And how would it be possible to flee from fashion?[56] The person who seeks to distance himself or herself from the prevailing fashion by deliberately wearing unmodern clothes remains completely under the dictates of fashion, simply because he or she is negating it. Such a person would possess as little real individualism as any 'fashion idiot', since one can no more become an independent individual by negating a norm than by affirming it.[57] For Simmel the ideal rather lies in a striving for relative independence based on recognizing fashion as a force in one's life, by which one is aware of the randomness of fashion and, via such a reflective relationship, does not simply surrender to the changes of fashion.

Gilles Lipovetsky claims that fashion 'has succeeded in turning the superficial into an instrument of salvation, into a goal of existence.'[58] Rather than condemn fashion as tyrannical, Lipovetsky stresses fashion as a realization of human autonomy in a world of surface.[59] He goes so far as to state: 'The fashion form reflects the final form of the democratization of minds and meanings.'[60] He claims that the increasing use of sportswear reflects an increasing demand for personal freedom, that the emphasis on youthfulness goes hand in hand with the democracy's emphasis on individualization and that jeans are a symbol of an individuality that has been liberated from social status.[61] But is individualization synonymous with democratization? A democracy must naturally have room for individual choices if it is to merit the term 'democracy', but it is not for that reason given that extreme egocentrism in its members – something Lipovetsky believes is the core of a world governed by fashions – produces a democratic gain. The philosopher Martha Nussbaum objects to Lipovetsky's view, arguing that the culture he praises is anything but a democratic culture of enlightenment, and that it does not consist of genuinely autonomous people but quite simply of slaves of fashion who are unable to connect to anything or anyone at all.[62] Here Lipovetsky would have answered that this culture consists of autonomous slaves of fashion, and that precisely this will produce a democratic gain. His point is that the more fashion gains ground, the more superficial we become, lessening social friction, so that a pluralistic democracy can function more and more painlessly. In short, if you give all your attention to a jacket from Prada, you will not bash in your neighbour's skull. As far as I know, no comparative surveys have been carried out on the relationship between fascination with fashion and the tendency to resort to violence. It is anything but obvious that the two things influence each other to any appreciable extent, although some recent thought-provoking works of fiction point in the opposite direction, including *American Psycho* and *Fight Club*. It is difficult to arrive at any well-founded conclusion here – except that Lipovetsky's assertion is not well-founded. Yet this is actually the argument he uses to honour his assertion that fashion is a great blessing for humanity.[63] Despite that, it is problematic to claim that a democracy functions better the less social friction it contains. Democracy needs friction. A democratic surplus has to be created, not just a frictionless indifference. A crucial obligation for a liberal democracy consists in encouraging democratic discourse in the public space, and this discourse does not function optimally when it glides too smoothly. Lipovetsky's fashion people are not political players who contribute to democracy. They fit better into Hermann Broch's description: 'where political thought is totally lacking . . . the aesthetic category comes more and more into the foreground', and this aesthetic category develops into 'life ornamentation and life decoration'.[64]

One can have an identity simply because certain things *mean* something for one – and conversely, it is one's identity that makes it possible to decide what has meaning for one and what does not.[65] In Bret Easton Ellis's novel *American Psycho* this is made clear by the identity-less Patrick Bateman being completely unable to grasp the difference between essential and non-essential differences: he completely lacks any bearings regarding values. This rebounds and thus reinforces his lack of identity. He is so utterly detached from everything and everyone that he, in a certain sense, is totally free – but this freedom is devoid of content. In that sense he is closely related to the fashion person described by Lipovetsky. This person is free in a way – Lipovetsky is right about that – but what sort of freedom are we dealing with here? It is a freedom from all traditions, from one's own past and from every life project that extends beyond the next change in fashion. It is a freedom from every deep conviction and a freedom from every binding relationship to another human being. But what is it a freedom *for*? This remains an open question. Lipovetsky's fashion person governs an absolutely negative freedom, but appears to lack any conception of positive freedom.[66] He has a freedom to realize himself but no positive definition of what sort of a self is to be realized. Such an individual is a dyed-in-the-wool Romantic, someone who always wants to become a different person than the one he (or she) is, but who will never become that person because he does not have any positive conception of who he wants to be.

Conclusion

Real life – full of imitations
Real life – I talk to you in codes
Real life – real imagination
Real life – I hide behind these clothes
Weeping Willows[1]

The fashion industry, in particular the large fashion houses, have been experiencing difficult years for some time now,[2] but the economic forecasts are that the market will sharply increase in future rather than decline.[3] From an aesthetic perspective, however, there are reasons for stating that fashion has never been less interesting than it is today. *Haute couture* has ceased to be a norm for mass fashion and can now mainly be considered to be advertising with artistic ambitions. It has done well as advertising, but only on rare occasions as art. The heyday of clothes fashion – the period during which it still appeared to be presenting something new – basically lasted for only a century, from the time Charles Frederick Worth opened his fashion house in Paris in 1857 until the 1960s. Since then the traditional replacement logic of fashion, by which something new is constantly replaced by something even newer, has itself been replaced by a logic of supplementation, where all styles become more or less contemporaneous and every style is endlessly recyclable.

What characterizes today's fashion is a stylistic pluralism that has hardly ever been stronger.[4] Stylistic pluralism is by no means a new phenomenon. In an article from 1916, Simmel notes that his age is 'styleless' because there is no predominant style but only a myriad of heterogeneous styles.[5] But we can safely state that this development has been radicalized since Simmel's time. It is basically self-evident that the pluralization of the life that characterizes modernity will be accompanied by a pluralization of fashion. Contrary to the Frankfurt School's fear of uniformity, the exact opposite would appear to have been the case – a hyper-differentiation. The spread of fashion has led to diversity not homogenization, to enormous stylistic variation rather than uniformity.

Pluralism in fashion does not necessarily make us any freer. Anne Hollander claims that 'the tyranny of fashion itself has in fact never been stronger than in this period of visual pluralism.'[6] This is not least due to the fact that all of us have been made *responsible* for the surface we present to the outside world. For Lipovetsky, fashion represents the opposite of tyranny: fashion promotes freedom rather than coercion. He rejoices where Baudrillard despairs, and considers fashion to be a productive game rather than a force that has deprived postmodern life of reality. The objection can of course be raised to Lipovetsky that even if the freedom to choose between brand X and brand Y, between two, three or four buttons on a suit, or between two lengths of skirt, is undeniably a form of freedom, it is one based on a choice that does not constitute any real difference. Despite this, we apparently allow ourselves to be convinced that these actually are important differences. Our consumption, at least, would seem to indicate we allow ourselves to be so.

Fashion has presented itself as something that could shape our lives. But, as Malcolm McLaren points out: 'Fashion doesn't have that power any more. It reached its peak when all those designers became orators and philosophers, when they began to believe that they could design their customers' lives as well as their clothes. Everybody waited for them to say something significant, but they never did.'[7] We can safely state that fashion functions relatively badly as a guide to life. What it can offer does not, despite everything, add all that much to our lives in the way of essential significance, and when the logic of fashion becomes the norm for the formation of identity, it has the opposite effect – it dissolves identity.

Simmel observed early on – a whole century ago – that fashion can be used as an indicator of the process of civilization, because an awareness of fashion indicates self-awareness, in the sense of ego-centrism, and that a swifter development in fashion indicates an increasing complexity of self-image, of self-identity. At the extreme of this development lies the completely decentralized subject. The pursuit of identity has then resulted dialectically in its opposite: the total dissolution of identity. That is perhaps where we are heading – but we have not got there yet.[8]

In my introduction I wrote that what had to be at the centre of a philosophical investigation of fashion was the *meaning* of fashion. I have attempted to uncover this meaning by studying the diffusion patterns of fashion, its logic and temporality, its relationship to body and language, its status as a commodity and as art and, not least, as an ideal for the construction of the self. The conclusion of all these studies can hardly be anything other than to say that fashion is a highly diverse phenomenon that pretends to have meaning, but in reality has meaning to only a very limited extent. It is always possible to say, as the fashion theorist Caroline Evans does, that fashion is capable of expressing the underlying interests circulating in culture, and that as such it is 'a route to unpleasant truths about the world'.[9] But what truths are these? That we cultivate surfaces, that we live in an increasingly fictionalized reality, that the constancy of our identities is steadily declining? In that case, fashion tells us truths that it has been perhaps the foremost driving force in realizing.

References

1
Introduction: A Philosophy of Fashion

1 Thomas Carlyle, *Sartor Resartus* (London, 1833–4).
2 Bret Easton Ellis, *Glamorama* (1999).
3 Cf. Jennifer Craik, *The Face of Fashion: Cultural Studies in Fashion* (London, 1994), p. 205.
4 Walter Benjamin, *Selected Writings*, vol. IV: *1938–1940*, trans. Edmund Jephcott et. al., ed. Howard Eiland and Michael W. Jennings (Cambridge, MA, 2003), p. 179.
5 Such accusations are by no means a new phenomenon. See, for example, Hegel's discussion of this term in G.W.F. Hegel, *Lectures on the History of Philosophy I*, trans. T. M. Knox (Lincoln and London, 1995), p. 42.
6 Huge numbers of histories of fashion have been written. One of the better ones, giving an account of fashion from the Middle Ages to the present day, is, in my opinion, Christopher Breward, *The Culture of Fashion: A New History of Fashionable Dress* (Manchester, 1995).
7 Adam Smith, *The Theory of Moral Sentiments* [1759] (Indianapolis, 1982), p. 195.
8 *Ibid.*, pp. 200–11.
9 Immanuel Kant, *Anthropology From a Pragmatic Point of View*, trans. Victor Lyle Dowdell (Carbondale and Edwardsville, IL, 1978), § 71, p. 148.
10 Novalis, *Fichte-Studien*, I/2: *Werke, Tagebücher und Briefe*

Friedrich von Hardenbergs (Darmstadt, 1999), p. 192.

11 Georg Simmel, *Gesamtausgabe*, x: *Philosophie der Mode* (Frankfurt am Main, 1989), p. 13.

12 Gilles Lipovetsky, *The Empire of Fashion: Dressing Modern Democracy*, ed. Catherine Porter (Princeton, NJ, 1994), p. 16. See also 'Fashion is a social logic independent of its content' (p. 227).

13 Anne Hollander, *Seeing through Clothes* (Berkeley, CA, 1975, rev. 1993), p. 350.

14 Elisabeth Wilson, *Adorned in Dreams: Fashion and Modernity* (London, 2003), p. 3.

15 Roland Barthes, *The Fashion System* (Berkeley, CA, 1983).

16 Ludwig Wittgenstein, *Philosophical Investigations*, trans. G.E.M. Anscombe (Oxford, 1968), p.32.

17 Lars Fr. H. Svendsen, *Hva er filosofi* (Oslo, 2003), p. 71.

18 Hans-Georg Gadamer, *Truth and Method* (London, 1975), p. 35.

19 Gadamer: 'What is Truth?', in *Hermeneutics and Truth*, ed. Brice R. Wachterhauser (Evanston, IL, 1994), pp. 40–41.

20 Simmel, *Philosophie der Mode*, p. 13.

21 Hegel, *Lectures on the History of Philosophy I*, p. 484.

22 Charles Taylor, *Sources of the Self: The Making of Modern Identity* (Cambridge, MA, 1989). This also applies to a number of other studies, e.g. Harvey Ferguson, *Modernity and Subjectivity: Body, Soul, Spirit* (Charlottesville, VA, 2000), Anthony J. Cascardi, *The Subject of Modernity* (Cambridge, 1992) and Daniel Shanahan, *Towards a Genealogy of Individualism* (Amherst, MA, 1992).

23 See Plato, *Hippias Maior*, 294a–b.

24 Kant, *Anthropology From a Pragmatic Point of View*, p. 148.

25 Quoted from the Introduction by Kerry McSweeney and Peter Sabor to Thomas Carlyle, *Sartor Resartus* (Oxford, 1987), p. xiii.

26 Carlyle, *Sartor Resartus*, p. 41.

27 *Ibid.*, pp. 57–8.

28 *Ibid.*, p. 30.

29 Hélène Cixous, 'Sonia Rykiel in Translation', in *On Fashion*, ed. Shari Benstock and Suzanne Ferris (New Brunswick, NJ, 1994), pp. 95–9.
30 Jay McInerney: *Model Behaviour* (New York, 1998), p. 31.

2
The Principle of Fashion: The New

1 Ezra Pound, *Make It New* (London, 1934).
2 Andy Warhol, THE *Philosophy of Andy Warhol (From* A *to* B *and Back Again)* (New York, 1975).
3 Christopher Breward, *The Culture of Fashion: A New History of Fashionable Dress* (Manchester, 1995), p. 171.
4 Friedrich Nietzsche, *Der Wanderer und sein Schatten* [1880], in *Kritische Studienausgabe*, II (Munich, 1988), p. 215.
5 Roland Barthes, *The Fashion System* (Berkeley, CA, 1983), p. 273.
6 Cf. Marc Froment-Meurice, *Solitudes: From Rimbaud to Heidegger* (Albany, NY, 1995), p. 23.
7 Gianni Vattimo, *The End of Modernity* (Baltimore, 1989), pp. 99ff.
8 Adolf Loos, *Spoken into the Void: Collected Essays, 1897–1900*, ed. J. O. Newman and J. H. Smith (Cambridge, MA, 1982), p. 53.
9 Cf. Adolf Loos, 'Ornament and Crime', in *Ornament and Crime: Selected Essays*, ed. Adolf Opel, trans. Michael Mitchell (Riverside, CA, 1998).
10 Loos, *Spoken into the Void*, p. 12.
11 Kant, *Anthropology From a Pragmatic Point of View*, § 71, p. 148.
12 *Ibid.* Kant agrees here with Adam Smith, who points out that there are no exterior objects that are so absurdly formed that fashion cannot make us like them (Adam Smith, *The Theory of Moral Sentiments* [1759], Indianapolis, 1982, p. 200).
13 Charles Baudelaire, 'The Painter of Modern Life' in *The Painter of Modern Life and Other Essays*, trans. Jonathan Mayne (London, 1964), pp. 32–3.
14 *Ibid.*, p. 12

15 *Ibid.*, p. 3. See also the following passage: 'All forms of beauty contain, as do all phenomena, something eternal and something fleeting, something absolute and something distinctive. Absolute and eternal beauty does not exist, or rather: it is only an abstraction, the foam on the general surface of the various forms of beauty. The *distinctive* element of beautiful comes from the passions – and since we have our distinctive passions, we also have our own beauty' (*ibid.*).

16 Concerning Mallarmé's work as a fashion editor, see, for example, Ulrich Lehmann, *Tigersprung: Fashion in Modernity* (Cambridge, MA, 2000), pp. 53–124.

17 Valéry, *Essays and aphorisms*, p. 108.

18 Roland Barthes, *The Pleasure of the Text*, trans. Richard Miller (New York, 1975), p. 40.

19 Rosalind E. Krauss, *The Originality of the Avant-Garde and Other Modernist Myths* (Cambridge, MA, 1985), p. 157.

20 *Ibid.*, p. 162.

21 Cf. James Breslin, *Mark Rothko: A Biography* (Chicago, 1993), p. 431.

22 The expression 'urge to innovate' has been taken from Boris Groys, *Über das Neue: Versuch einer Kulturökonomie* (Munich, 1992), p. 10.

23 *Ibid.*, p. 12.

24 As Adorno points out, this leads in a certain sense to everything new being identical simply by virtue of being this one thing, i.e. new: 'The category of the new is an abstract negation of the lasting and as such coincides with it: the weakness both share is the invariant quality about them.' (Adorno, *Estetisk teori*, p. 467).

25 Cf. Michael J. Wolf, *The Entertainment Economy* (Harmondsworth, 1999), p. 293.

26 Here, however, subcultural fashions are partly an exception, as they frequently have the nature of being direct comments on society. But because some subcultural fashions have this characteristic, it does not mean that all fashions do. As

shown in chapter Four below, subcultural fashions often have a larger 'propositional content' than other fashions, but we also see that mass fashion is, broadly speaking, devoid of it, and that mass fashion effectively empties subcultural fashions of any content when it absorbs them.

27 Jean Baudrillard, *For a Critique of the Political Economy of the Sign* (New York, 1980), p. 79.
28 Cf. Breward, *The Culture of Fashion*, p. 19.
29 Cf. Anne Hollander, *Sex and Suits: The Evolution of Modern Dress* (Berkeley, CA, 1994), p. 166.
30 Milan Kundera, *Slowness*, trans. Linda Asher (London, 1996), pp. 34–5.
31 Barthes, *The Fashion System*, p. 273.
32 Cf. Gilles Lipovetsky, *The Empire of Fashion: Dressing Modern Democracy*, ed. Catherine Porter (Princeton, NJ, 1994), p. 233.
33 Benjamin, *Selected Writings*, vol. IV: *1938–1940*, p. 179.
34 This tendency undoubtedly applies to art (cf. Lars Fr. H. Svendsen, *Kunst*, Oslo, 2000, pp. 106), but to an even greater extent to fashion.
35 Benjamin Buchloh, 'Conversation with Andy Warhol', in *The Duchamp Effect*, ed. M. Buskirk and M. Nixon (Cambridge, MA, 1996), p. 44.
36 Thomas More: *Utopia*, trans. and ed. Paul Turner (Harmondsworth, 1983), p. 75.
37 *Ibid.*, pp. 78–9.
38 Groys, *Über das Neue*, p. 45.
39 Walter Benjamin, *Gesammelte Schriften*, V: *Das Passagen-Werk* (Frankfurt am Main, 1991), B4, 4.

3
The Origins and Spread of Fashion

1 Richard Steele, *The Tender Husband* [1705], ed. Calhoun Winton (London, 1967).
2 Martin Gore, 'The Sun and the Rainfall', on Depeche Mode,

A Broken Frame [1982] (Reprise 23751).

3 A theory that has been aired in recent times is that of so-called 'memetics'; see in particular Richard Dawkins, *The Selfish Gene* (2nd edn, Oxford, 1989), pp. 189–201, and Susan Blackmore, *The Meme Machine* (Oxford, 1999). However, I believe I have shown elsewhere why the memetic theory does not work, and do not intend to revisit it here (cf. Lars Fr. H. Svendsen, *Mennesket, moralen og genene*, Oslo, 2001, pp. 106–17).

4 One of the most detailed studies of such laws is Frances Elisabeth Baldwin, *Sumptuary Legislation and Personal Regulation in England* (Baltimore, 1926).

5 See, for example, Diana Crane, *Fashion and its Social Agendas: Class, Gender and Identity in Clothing* (Chicago, 2000), pp. 3ff.

6 This thought is so pervasive in various theories about fashion, especially in sociology, that it is even found in such unorthodox thinkers as Jean Baudrillard in his early work. See Jean Baudrillard, *The Consumer Society: Myths and Structures* (London, 1970, 2/1988), pp. 62ff.

7 Smith, *The Theory of Moral Sentiments*, p. 64.

8 Kant, *Anthropology From a Pragmatic Point of View*, p. 148.

9 Herbert Spencer develops this idea in a number of his writings, but the best and most comprehensive account is given in *The Principles of Sociology*, II/4 (London, 1879). For an easy-to-read account of Spencer's fashion sociology, see Michael Carter, *Fashion Classics from Carlyle to Barthes* (Oxford, 2003), chap. 2.

10 Jorge Luis Borges, *The Total Library: Non-fiction, 1922–1986* (Harmondsworth, 1999), p. 518.

11 Thorstein Veblen, 'The Economic Theory of Women's Dress', in *Essays in our Changing Order*, ed. Leon Ardzrooni (New York, 1964), p. 72.

12 Thorstein Veblen, *The Theory of the Leisure Class* [1899] (Amherst, NY, 1998), p. 36.

13 Concerning this concept, see in particular *ibid.*, chap. 4.
14 *Ibid.*, pp. 103ff.
15 *Ibid.*, p. 115.
16 *Ibid.*, chapter 6.
17 *Ibid.*, p. 177.
18 Georg Simmel, *Gesamtausgabe*, X: *Philosophie der Mode* (Frankfurt am Main, 1989), pp. 9ff.
19 *Ibid.*, p. 31.
20 Here Darwin's assertion could also be mentioned that 'the fashions of savages are more permanent than ours' (Charles Darwin, *The Descent of Man, and Selection in Relation to Sex* [1871], Amherst, NY, 1998, p. 605).
21 Simmel, *Philosophie der Mode*, pp. 11, 13.
22 *Ibid.*, p. 32.
23 Georg Simmel, 'Die Mode', in *Gesamtausgabe*, XIV (Frankfurt am Main, 1989), p. 196.
24 Gabriel de Tarde, *Les lois de l'imitation* (Paris, 1890; trans. Elsie Clews Parsons, Gloucester, MA, 1962), p. 215.
25 Anne Hollander, *Sex and Suits: The Evolution of Modern Dress* (Berkeley, CA, 1994), p. 7.
26 This is in the process of changing. Most major works on fashion normally contain at least one chapter on men's fashion. A number of works have also now been written that specifically focus on the subject.
27 Hollander, *Sex and Suits*, p. 9.
28 Cf. Jennifer Craik, *The Face of Fashion: Cultural Studies in Fashion* (London, 1994), p. 176.
29 See, for example, Kåre Tønnesson, *Revolusjonen som rystet Europa: Frankrike 1789–1815* (Oslo, 1989), p. 10.
30 It should also be noted here that both *denim* and *jeans* are of American origin, derived from the European terms 'Serge de Nîmes' for the material and 'Genuese' (i.e. from Genoa) for the cut.
31 Cf. Fred Davis, *Fashion, Culture, and Identity* (Chicago, 1992), pp. 68ff.

32 Andy Warhol: THE *Philosophy of Andy Warhol (From* A *to* B *and Back Again)* (New York, 1975), p. 101.

33 What is to be considered *haute couture* and what not is basically a matter of preference. But the official requirements are as follows: in order to satisfy the criteria for *haute couture* a fashion designer must have at least 20 seamstresses employed and show at least two collections with 75 creations each year – and these creations must be hand-sewn and made to measure.

34 See Diana Crane, *Fashion and its Social Agendas: Class, Gender and Identity in Clothing* (Chicago, 2000), pp. 26–66.

35 Bourdieu emphasizes that, where it is vital for Kant's aesthetics of autonomy to eliminate the functionality of the object if it is to be the object of a genuine judgment of taste, 'popular' taste expects the exact opposite, i.e. the object must have a functionality, even if it is only a functional *sign* in a painting (Pierre Bourdieu, *La distinction: Critique sociale du jugement*, Paris, 1979; trans. Richard Nice, Cambridge, MA, 1984). Perhaps we can say that allegedly disinterested taste is only a reflection of the interests of a particular social class.

36 Crane, *Fashion and its Social Agendas*, pp. 58ff.

37 See in particular Bourdieu, *La distinction*. I am using the Norwegian edition: *Distinksjonen*, trans. Annick Prieur (Oslo, 1995).

38 Bourdieu, *Distinksjonen*, p. 99.

39 *Ibid.*, p. 249.

40 *Ibid.*, p. 218.

41 Another interesting similarity between Veblen and Bourdieu that ought to be examined further is the relationship between Bourdieu's concept of 'habitus' and Veblen's concept of 'life habits' (Veblen, *Theory of the Leisure Class*, pp. 106ff, 195, 221), which have a number of similarities.

42 Pierre Bourdieu, 'Social Space and Symbolic Power', *Sociological Theory*, I (1989), p. 20.

43 Veblen, *Theory of the Leisure Class*, p. 115.

44 Colin Campbell has therefore criticized Veblen for confusing

two types of explanation – explanations of purpose and functionalist explanations – in his account of conspicuous consumption (Colin Campbell, 'Conspicuous Confusion? A Critique of Veblen's Theory of Conspicuous Consumption', *Sociological Theory*, 1995). It must at least be conceded that Veblen does not always distinguish between these two types of explanation and make clear precisely which type of explanation he is giving.

45 See, for example: 'The new lower middle classes are predisposed to wholeheartedly take part in landing others with the lifestyle the new middle class stands for, as, when all is said and done, the position of the new middle class is the real aim of the lower middle classes' own aspirations and a probable terminus for their own career. [. . .] These lower middle classes are ready to play the role of intermediary in order to draw into the consumption and competition race precisely those they themselves are trying at any price to distinguish themselves from' (Bourdieu, *Distinksjonen*, p. 174).

46 In order to escape 'economism' as the basis of symbolic capitalism, Bourdieu refers to a number of 'uneconomic' practices where exchange takes place. He claims that 'economism is a form of ethnocentrism' (Pierre Bourdieu, *The Logic of Practice*, Cambridge, 1990, p. 112) because it treats economies as if they were variants of modern, capitalist economy. Such a model, however, is unable to explain a number of forms of exchange.

47 Cf. Bourdieu, *Distinksjonen*, pp. 48–9.

48 *Ibid.*, p. 219.

49 *Ibid.*, p. 36.

50 *Ibid.*, p. 73.

51 *Ibid.*, p. 52

52 *Ibid.*, p. 45.

53 *Ibid.*, p. 38.

54 *Ibid.*, p. 126.

55 Herbert Blumer, 'Fashion: From Class Differentiation to

Collective Selection', *Sociological Quarterly*, x (1969), p. 281.

56 As the sociologist Fred Davis points out, it is also a problem that Blumer's theory does not take into account the entire apparatus that lies behind the launching and dissemination of a style – designers, fashion houses, trend researchers and press (Davis, *Fashion, Culture, and Identity*, pp. 115–20).

57 See, for example, Anne Hollander, *Seeing through Clothes* (Berkeley, CA, 1975, rev. 1993), p. 351.

58 Eric Hobsbawm, *The Age of Extremes* (London 1995), p. 178.

59 Cf. Davis, *Fashion, Culture, and Identity*, p. 135.

60 See Crane, *Fashion and its Social Agendas*, p. 135.

61 Gilles Lipovetsky, *The Empire of Fashion: Dressing Modern Democracy*, ed. Catherine Porter (Princeton, NJ, 1994), p. 97.

62 Cf. Anne Hollander, *Feeding the Eye* (Berkeley, CA, 2000), p. 112.

63 Lipovetsky, *The Empire of Fashion*, p. 41.

4
Fashion and Language

1 Martin Amis, *Other People* (London, 1981).

2 Cf. Christopher Breward, *The Culture of Fashion: A New History of Fashionable Dress* (Manchester, 1995), p. 87.

3 Alison Lurie, *The Language of Clothes* (New York, 1981, 2/2000), p. 4.

4 *Ibid.*, p. 5.

5 *Ibid.*, pp. 35–6.

6 *Ibid.*, pp. 244–5. It must be admitted here that it is James Laver's assertion that is being passed on by Lurie, although she does give him her support.

7 Another problem about Lurie's book is that she seems to have a view of language that is akin to the discredited idea theory of language, to which she does, admittedly, give a psychoanalytical twist. According to idea theory, linguistic expressions gain meaning by being associated with ideas in

human consciousness that are independent of language. This theory, which was advocated by British empiricists in particular, encountered insuperable difficulties in providing an account of how language works, and most contemporary language philosophy takes a critique of this theory as its point of departure. (For a more detailed account of idea theory and the problems involved in it, see Lars Fr. H. Svendsen and Simo Säätelä, *Det sanne, det gode og det skjønne*, Oslo, 2004, pp. 102ff.)

8 Fred Davis, *Fashion, Culture, and Identity* (Chicago, 1992), p. 7.

9 Roland Barthes, *The Fashion System* (Berkeley, CA, 1983), p. XI.

10 *Ibid.*, p. 8.

11 *Ibid.*, pp. 213–14.

12 *Ibid.*, p. 236.

13 *Ibid.*, pp. 287–8.

14 *Ibid.*, p. 263.

15 Here it could perhaps be argued that such an approach is guilty of what New Criticism called 'the intentional fallacy', where the point was that the meaning of a work of art cannot be explained by referring to the intentions of the artist, as it is the work itself that has meaning (cf. W. K. Wimsatt and Monroe C. Beardsley, 'The Intentional Fallacy', in *The Verbal Icon: Studies in the Meaning of Poetry*, Lexington, KY, 1982). On the other hand, it is a good idea to be critical of some of the assumptions made by the New Critics, e.g. that the work ought to be considered a completely autonomous entity.

16 Broch, *Hofmansthal og hans tid*, ed. Sverre Dahl (Oslo, 1987) p. 121.

17 Diana Crane, *Fashion and its Social Agendas: Class, Gender and Identity in Clothing* (Chicago, 2000), pp. 242–3. Crane has probably taken the distinction between 'open' and 'closed' texts from Umberto Eco, *The Role of the Reader: Explorations in the Semiotics of Texts* (Bloomington, IN, 1979).

18 Anne Hollander, *Seeing through Clothes* (Berkeley, CA, 1975, rev. 1993), pp. 365–90.

19 *The Economist*, 4 March 2004.

20 David Muggleton, *Inside Subculture: The Postmodern Meaning of Style* (Oxford, 2000), pp. 47–8.

5
Fashion and the Body

1 Bret Easton Ellis, *Glamorama* (New York, 1999).

2 Andy Warhol, *THE Philosophy of Andy Warhol (From A to B and Back Again)* (New York, 1975).

3 Jennifer Saunders, 'Magazine', *Absolutely Fabulous*, BBC TV (10 December 1992).

4 This quite widespread view has been advanced in large sections of the recent literature about the self. A book that dealt with this theme relatively early on from a social-scientific point of view, and which is still up to the mark, is Bryan S. Turner, *The Body and Society* (Oxford, 1984).

5 Cf. Susan Bordo, 'Reading the Slender Body', in *Body and Flesh: A Philosophical Reader* (Oxford, 1998), p. 291.

6 Jean Baudrillard, *The Consumer Society: Myths and Structures* (London, 1970, 2/1988), p. 129.

7 Oscar Wilde, 'A Few Maxims for the Instruction of the Over-educated', in *Complete Works of Oscar Wilde* (London, 1966), p. 1203.

8 Cf. Harvey Ferguson, *Modernity and Subjectivity: Body, Soul, Spirit* (Charlottesville, VA, 2000), p. 23.

9 G.W.F. Hegel, *Aesthetics: Lectures on Fine Art II*, trans. E. S. Haldane (Lincoln and London, 1995), p. 747.

10 Hegel, *Lectures on the History of Philosophy I*, p. 484.

11 Cf. Colin McDowell, ed., *The Pimlico Companion to Fashion: A Literary Anthology* (London, 1998), p. 387.

12 See for example Hélène Cixous, 'Sonia Rykiel in Translation', in *On Fashion*, ed. Shari Benstock and Suzanne Ferris (New

Brunswick, NJ, 1994), pp. 95–9.

13 Anne Hollander, *Seeing through Clothes* (Berkeley, CA, 1975, rev. 1993), pp. 83–156.

14 *Ibid.*, p. 87.

15 Cf. Norbert Elias, *Über den Prozess der Zivilisation: Sosiogenetische und psychogenetische Untersuchungen*, I (Frankfurt am Main, 1997), pp. 316ff.

16 Mario Perniola, 'Between Clothing and Nudity', in *Fragments for a History of the Human Body*, ed. Michel Feher and others (New York, 1989), p. 237.

17 Hollander, *Seeing through Clothes*, pp. 83–156.

18 Cf. Mark C. Taylor, *Hiding* (Chicago, 1997), p. 185.

19 For a classic example of such an objection to clothes fashion, see Arthur Schopenhauer, *Sämtliche Werke*, v: *Parerga und Paralipomena II* (Frankfurt am Main, 1986), pp. 683–4.

20 Baudelaire, 'The Painter of Modern Life', pp. 32–3.

21 Charles Baudelaire, *Intimate Journals*, trans. Christopher Isherwood (London, 1949), p 25.

22 *Ibid.*, p. 26.

23 Baudelaire, 'The Painter of Modern Life', p. 33.

24 Carlyle, *Sartor Resartus*, Book I, chapters IX and X.

25 Georg Simmel, *Gesamtausgabe*, X: *Philosophie der Mode* (Frankfurt am Main, 1989), p. 36.

26 *Elle*, March 1991.

27 Musil, *Mannen uten egenskaper*, vol. I, p. 20.

28 NTB News, 9 July 2004.

29 Karl Kraus, *Aphorismen: Sprüche und Widersprüche* (Frankfurt am Main, 1986), p. 24.

30 Erling Dokk Holm, *Fra Gud til Gucci* (Oslo, 2004), p. 148.

31 See, for example, Kathryn Pauly Morgan, 'Women and the Knife: Cosmetic Surgery and the Colonization of Women's Bodies', in *Body and Flesh: A Philosophical Reader*, ed. Donn Welton (Oxford, 1998), pp. 325–47.

32 For an account of body modification as fashion, see, for example, Paul Sweetman, 'Anchoring the (Postmodern) Self?

Body Modification, Fashion and Identity', in *Body Modification*, ed. Mike Featherstone (London, 2000).

33 Cf. Jennifer Craik, *The Face of Fashion: Cultural Studies in Fashion* (London, 1994), p. 153.

34 Harold Koda, *Extreme Beauty: The Body Transformed* (New York, 2001), p. 13.

35 Valerie Steele, 'The Corset: Fashion and Eroticism', *Fashion Theory*, II (1999), p. 473.

36 Baudrillard, *America*, trans. Chris Turner (London and New York, 1988) p. 38.

37 Cf. Craik, *The Face of Fashion*, p. 84. This can of course partially be explained by the fact that the average American body has become heavier.

38 Anthony Giddens, *Modernity and Self-Identity: Self and Identity in the Late Modern Age* (Cambridge, 1991), p. 7.

39 In *Modesty in Dress: An Inquiry into the Fundamentals of Fashion* (London, 1969), James Laver launched the theory of the 'changing erogenous zone', according to which a certain part of the female body is accentuated during a certain period, whereas another part is chosen during a different period. So far, Laver's theory is unproblematic, but the explanation he gives is more doubtful. He claims that a constant change of erogenous zones is necessary for men not to get bored. Firstly, this means that women are completely at the mercy of the male gaze, i.e. women don sexy clothes exclusively in order to attract men, which there are good reasons to doubt. Secondly, it would explain only changes in women's fashion and not men's fashion – the converse would also have to be true, that men's fashion changes so that women will not become bored. If that were so, it is strange that men's fashion has generally speaking undergone only relatively small, subtle changes from the early nineteenth century onwards.

40 Cf. Elisabeth Wilson, *Adorned in Dreams: Fashion and Modernity* (2nd edn, London, 2003), p. 131.

41 The following reflections on the nature of breasts is to a

great extent based on Koda, *Extreme Beauty*, pp. 50–69.

42 See also Hollander, *Seeing through Clothes*, p. 98.

43 See, for example, John Curra, *The Relativity of Deviance* (London, 2000), esp. pp. 1–38.

44 The search for such universal standards has been popular in parts of socio-biology and evolution psychology. See, for example, Steven Pinker, *How the Mind Works* (Harmondsworth, 1998), pp. 483–7, and Edward O. Wilson, *Consilience: The Unity of Knowledge* (London, 1998), pp. 256ff.

45 Susannah Frankel, *Visionaries: Interviews with Fashion Designers* (London, 2001), p. 154.

6
Fashion and Art

1 Pet Shop Boys, 'Flamboyant', *Pop Art* (2003), Parlophone 5938842.

2 See Nancy J. Troy, *Couture Culture: A Study in Modern Art and Fashion* (Cambridge, MA, 2003), chapter 1.

3 Quoted from Troy, *Couture Culture*, p. 47.

4 Susannah Frankel, *Visionaries: Interviews with Fashion Designers* (London, 2001), p. 35. Margiela is by no means the only one of the most avant-garde fashion designers to reject the idea of being called an artist. Another example is Kawakubo (*ibid.*, p. 160). Angela McRobbie, on the other hand, interviewed a number of English fashion designers who considered themselves, and wished to be considered, as artists (Angela McRobbie, *British Fashion Design: Rag Trade or Image Industry?*, London, 1998, p. 6).

5 Cf. Fred Davis, *Fashion, Culture, and Identity* (Chicago, 1992), pp. 126–7. There are, of course, exceptions, such as Holly Brubach, but we are dealing precisely with exceptions. A solid selection of Brubach's articles have been published as *A Dedicated Follower of Fashion* (London, 1999).

6 Pierre Bourdieu, 'Haute Couture and Haute Culture', 'But Who Created the "Creators"?', in *Sociology in Question* (London, 1993), pp. 132–8, 139–48.

7 See, in particular, Troy, *Couture Culture*.

8 To mention some such exhibitions: *Fashion and Surrealism* (Victoria and Albert Museum, London, 1988), *Streetstyle* (Victoria and Albert Museum, London, 1994), *Il tempo e le mode* (Florence Biennale, 1996 – this exhibition was then shown under the title *Art/Fashion* at the Solomon R. Guggenheim Museum, New York) and *Addressing the Century: A Hundred Years of Art and Fashion* (Hayward Gallery, London, 1998).

9 On the use of art in advertising contexts, see James B. Twitchell, *Adcult USA: The Triumph of Advertising in American Culture* (New York, 1996), pp. 179–228.

10 Cf. Chris Townsend, *Rapture: Art's Seduction by Fashion since 1970* (London, 2002), pp. 45ff; this is one of the better studies on the relationship between art and fashion.

11 See, for example, T. J. Clark, *Farewell to an Idea: Episodes from a History of Modernism* (New Haven, CT, 1994).

12 Quoted from Townsend, *Rapture*, p. 96.

13 Cf. Caroline Evans, *Fashion at the Edge: Spectacle, Modernity and Deathliness* (New Haven, CT, 2003), pp. 69–70.

14 Or as Siri Meyer puts it: 'From being a means to mark and maintain social positions, *haute couture* has become part of the sign economy.' (Siri Meyer, 'Kledd for demokrati', in *Varene tar makten*, ed. Erling Dokk Holm and Siri Meyer, Oslo, 2001, p. 108.)

15 For a readable account of this trend in fashion, see Rebecca Arnold, *Fashion, Desire and Anxiety: Image and Morality in the 20th Century* (London, 2001).

16 For an account of this 'scandal', see Evans, *Fashion at the Edge*, p. 19.

17 *Walter Benjamin: Selected Writings*, III: *1935–1938*, ed. Howard Eiland and Michael W. Jennings (New York, 2002).

18 Cf. Frankel, *Visionaries*, p. 16.

19 *Ibid.*, p. 19.

20 Cf. Nathalie Khan, 'Catwalk Politics', in *Fashion Cultures: Theories, Explanations and Analyses*, ed. Stella Bruzzi and Pamela Church Gibson (London, 2000), p. 118.

21 Quoted from Naomi Klein, *No Logo* (London, 2000), p. 63.

22 Cf. Judith Watt, ed., *The Penguin Book of Twentieth-Century Fashion Writing* (Harmondsworth, 1999), p. 244.

23 Walter Benjamin, 'A Small History of Photography', in *One-Way Street and Other Writings*, trans. Edmund Jephcott and Kingsley Shorter (London, 1985), pp. 254–5.

24 Not least for that reason, a central characteristic of much of contemporary criticism of consumption has consisted of showing what production relations actually lie behind the commodities we buy. See for example Klein, *No Logo*, chapters 9–11.

25 Cf. Elliott Smedley, 'Escaping to Reality: Fashion Photography in the 1990s', in *Fashion Cultures*, ed. Bruzzi and Gibson.

26 Anne Hollander, *Seeing through Clothes* (Berkeley, CA, 1975, rev. 1993), p. 311.

27 Suzy Menkes, 'Playing to the Galleries: Wannabe Art', *International Herald Tribune*, 13 October 1998.

28 Cf. Adorno: *Estetisk teori*, ed. Arild Linnberg (Oslo, 1998), p. 39.

29 Immanuel Kant, *The Critique of Judgement* (Oxford, 1986), § 16, p. 72.

30 I have dealt with this at greater depth in Lars Fr. H. Svendsen, *Kunst* (Oslo, 2000), pp. 112–13.

31 Zandra Rhodes, 'Is Fashion a True Art Form?', *The Observer*, 13 July 2003.

32 Khan, 'Catwalk Politics', p. 123.

33 Clement Greenberg, 'Toward a Newer Laocoön', in *Art in Theory, 1900–1990*, ed. Charles Harrison and Paul Wood (Oxford, 1992), p. 556.

34 Sung Bok Kim, 'Is Fashion Art?', *Fashion Theory*, I (1998).

35 This is my main assertion in Svendsen, *Kunst*. See, in

particular, chapters 1 and 6.

36 Oscar Wilde: 'Pen, Pencil and Poison: a Study in Green', in *Complete Works of Oscar Wilde* (London, 1966), p. 997.

37 Adorno: *Estetisk teori*, p. 310.

38 *Ibid.*, p. 333.

39 Adorno also writes: 'Fashion is art's permanent admission that it is not what it pretends to be and what in relation to its idea it must be' (*ibid.*, p. 543). Here it is implied that there is an idea, a norm, for what art shall be, and Adorno also claims that art 'cannot satisfy its concept' (*ibid.*, p. 103). I would assert that art no longer has a concept to fulfil, that it has lost its concept, and therefore also the assignment to flesh out this concept. I have explained my position in more detail in Svendsen, *Kunst*, chapter 6.

40 Adorno: *Estetisk teori*, p. 543.

41 Cf. Ulrich Lehmann, *Tigersprung: Fashion in Modernity* (Cambridge, MA, 2000), p. 348.

7
Fashion and Consumption

1 The Clash, 'Lost in the Supermarket', *London Calling* (1979), Epic 36328.

2 Bret Easton Ellis, *Glamorama* (New York, 1999).

3 Jennifer Saunders, 'Birthday', *Absolutely Fabulous*, BBC TV (17 December 1992).

4 In this chapter the two Norwegian words *forbruk* and *konsum* have both been translated as 'consumption', as they were used only for linguistic variation.

5 See, for example, Zygmunt Bauman, 'From the Work Ethic to the Aesthetic of Consumption', *The Bauman Reader* (Oxford, 2001), p. 312. On boredom and consumption see also Peter N. Stearns, *Consumerism in World History: The Global Transformation of Desire* (London, 2001), pp. 22–3. Not many empirical studies have, by the way, been carried out on the

relationship between boredom and fashion consciousness, but the small amount of existing material would indicate a connection; cf. Cathryn M. Staudak and Jane E. Workman, 'Fashion Groups, Gender, and Boredom Proneness', *International Journal of Consumer Studies*, I (2004).

6 Manuel Castells, *The Network Society* (Oxford, 1996), I, p. 443.

7 Cf. Frode Nyeng, 'Den postmoderne forbrukeren – grenseløs frihet og smertefull individualisme', in Trond Blindheim, Thor Øyvind Jensen and Frode Nyeng, *Forbrukeren: Helt, skurk eller offer?* (Oslo, 2000).

8 Let me mention a major empirical survey from Great Britain that was published in 1992. In it, Peter Lunt and Sonia Livingstone found that the normal way average consumers used commodities, and not least their symbolic values, was of relevance for their construction of identity. These consumers were, however, not a completely homogeneous group and were divided into five categories: (1) alternative shoppers (12%), who bought second-hand clothes, went to flea-markets, etc; (2) routine shoppers (31%), who do not experience any particular pleasure or displeasure about shopping, but do it as part of their daily routine; (3) leisure shoppers (24%), who are close to the stereotype of the 'postmodern' consumer and who consider shopping an important part of life; (4) cautious shoppers (15%), who like to shop but are more interested in the actual products than the act of buying; (5) clever shoppers (18%), who like to shop but are mostly interested in getting everything as cheaply as possible (Peter Lunt and Sonia Livingstone: *Mass Consumption and Personal Identity: Everyday Economic Experience*, Buckingham, 1992, pp. 89–94). We can see that only a quarter of shoppers directly fit the image of the 'postmodern' consumer, while the other categories do so to greatly varying extents. Given the increase in private consumption of 40–50 per cent since this study was published, there are, however, reasons to assume that the group of 'leisure shoppers' has considerably increased.

9 It is not least extremely difficult to find clear patterns in the relation between income and clothes consumption. The percentage of income used on clothing has varied a great deal when it comes to economy, geography (both between different countries and between urban and rural areas), time, age, etc. In short, there is a set of variables with so great a variation that it is highly problematic to say anything general. In the course of the last century people have spent more and more money on clothes – with a marked increase in consumption, not least during the past few decades – but this has at the same time made up a diminishing amount of people's earnings. Generally speaking, clothes have become cheaper. Mass-produced trousers or shirts have never cost so little, compared to the average income in the population. Brand items, on the other hand, have not become significantly cheaper.

10 Daniel Miller, *Material Culture and Mass Consumption* (Oxford, 1987).

11 See in particular Daniel Miller: *A Theory of Shopping* (Ithaca, NY, 1988).

12 Cf. George Ritzer, *Enchanting a Disenchanted World: Revolutionizing the Means of Consumption* (London, 1999), p. 194.

13 Bauman, 'From the Work Ethic to the Aesthetic of Consumption', p. 330.

14 Mary Douglas and Baron Isherwood, *The World of Goods: Towards an Anthropology of Consumption* (London, 1979), p. 12.

15 Cf. Mark C. Taylor, *Hiding* (Chicago, 1997), p. 125.

16 Gilles Lipovetsky, *The Empire of Fashion: Dressing Modern Democracy*, ed. Catherine Porter (Princeton, NJ, 1994), p. 145.

17 Colin Campbell, *The Romantic Ethic and the Spirit of Modern Consumerism* (Blackwell, Oxford), 1989.

18 *Ibid.*, p. 227.

19 Friedrich Schlegel, *Critical Fragments*, in *Lucinde and the Fragments*, ed. Peter Firchow (Minneapolis, 1971), § 47, p. 149.

20 This point is also underlined by Charles Taylor, *Sources of the Self: The Making of Modern Identity* (Cambridge, MA, 1989), p. 458.

21 Campbell, *The Romantic Ethic and the Spirit of Modern Consumerism*, p. 95.

22 Cf. Zygmunt Bauman, *Intimations of Postmodernity* (London, 1992), p. 51.

23 Kalle Lasn, *Culture Jam* (New York, 1999), p. xi.

24 Michel de Certeau, *The Practice of Everyday Life* (Berkeley, CA, 1984).

25 Cf. Lipovetsky, *The Empire of Fashion*, p. 80.

26 Vance Packard, *The Hidden Persuaders* (New York, 1957).

27 See, for example, Naomi Wolf, *The Beauty Myth* (New York, 1991).

28 Frederic Jameson, *Postmodernism; or, The Cultural Logic of Late Capitalism* (Durham, NC, 1991), p. 44.

29 Rob Shields, 'The Logic of the Mall', in *The Socialness of Things: Essays on the Socio-Semiotics of Objects*, ed. S. M. Riggins (New York, 1994).

30 Ian Woodward, Michael Emmison and Philip Smith, 'Consumerism, Disorientation and Postmodern Space: a Modest Test of an Immodest Theory', *British Journal of Sociology*, LI/2 (2000), pp. 339–54.

31 Georg Simmel, *Gesamtausgabe*, VI: *Philosophie des Geldes* (Frankfurt am Main, 1989).

32 Simmel: 'Storbyene og åndslivet', pp. 99–100.

33 Simmel, *Philosophie des Geldes*, pp. 633–4.

34 Giacomo Leopardi, *Moral Tales*, vol. I, trans. Patrick Creagh (Manchester, 1983), pp. 51–2.

35 See, in particular, Simmel, 'Der Begriff und die Tragödie der Kultur', *Gesamtausgabe*, XIV (Frankfurt am Main, 1989), pp. 385–416.

36 Simmel: 'Storbyene og åndslivet', p. 100.

37 Bourdieu: *Distinksjonen*, p. 101.

38 Jean Baudrillard, *The System of Objects*, trans. James Benedict

(London and New York, 1996), p. 200.

39 Jean Baudrillard, *The Consumer Society: Myths and Structures* (London, 1970, 2/1988), p. 116.

40 Cf. Russell Belk, 'Possessions and the Extended Self', *Journal of Consumer Research*, xv (1988).

41 Nancy J. Troy, *Couture Culture: A Study in Modern Art and Fashion* (Cambridge, MA, 2003), p. 231.

42 Debord: *The Society of the Spectacle* (New York, 1995), § 193.

43 Troy, *Couture Culture.*

44 *Ibid.*, p. 25.

45 *Ibid.*, pp. 232ff.

46 David Boyle, *Authenticity, Brands, Fakes, Spin and the Lust for Real Life* (London, 2003), p. 46.

47 Erling Dokk Holm, *Fra Gud til Gucci* (Oslo, 2004), p. 18.

48 For such a survey of jeans, see Susan Auty and Richard Elliot, 'Social Identity and the Meaning of Fashion Brands', *European Advances in Consumer Research*, III (1998).

49 Cf. Boyle, *Authenticity, Brands, Fakes, Spin and the Lust for Real Life*, pp. 28–9.

50 Admittedly Bourdieu has a different, more complex theory of social classes than Veblen or Simmel (Cf. Bourdieu, *La distinction*), but I do not even so see this changing the decisive point, namely that Bourdieu's theory is too strongly linked to a class perspective of consumption to capture the most central aspects of so-called 'postmodern' consumption.

51 Harvie Ferguson, 'Watching the World Go Round: Atrium Culture and the Psychology of Shopping', *Lifestyle Shopping: The Subject of Consumption*, ed. Rob Shields (London, 1992), p. 38.

52 Cf. Robert Bocock, *Consumption* (London, 1993), p. 51.

53 Max Horkheimer and Theodor W. Adorno, *Dialectic of Enlightenment*, trans. John Cumming (London, 1973), pp. 124–5.

54 John Fiske, *Understanding Popular Culture* (London, 1989), p. 37.

55 Much has been written about the role of style in subcultures.

A classic in this area is Dick Hebdige, *Subculture: The Meaning of Style* (London, 1979, rev. 1988). For a more up-to-date account that is critical of Hebdige on central issues, see David Muggleton, *Inside Subculture: The Postmodern Meaning of Style* (Oxford, 2000).

56 Hebdige, *Subculture*, p. 103.

57 *Ibid.*, pp. 113ff.

58 When one reads hip management books from the past ten to fifteen years – whether they are called *Funky Business*, *The Dream Society* or *Corporate Religion* – one is struck by how traditional the idea content is. Old *countercultural* ideals are recirculated, with the emphasis on unconventionality, imagination, self-realization, revolution, etc. One difference, of course, is that these books are pro-capitalist, while the former countercultural ideas tended to be the exact opposite. But the main point is that in our consumer society classic counterculture has been incorporated into the consumer culture and stands there as the main supplier. Individualism, personal freedom, imagination – these are sales commodities more than anything else.

59 Thomas Frank, 'Why Johnny Can't Dissent', in *Commodify your Dissent*, ed. Thomas Frank and Matt Weiland (New York, 1997).

60 See, for example, Joseph Heath, 'The Structure of Hip Consumerism', *Philosophy and Social Criticism*, VI (2001).

61 Don DeLillo, *Cosmopolis* (New York, 2003), p. 104.

62 Hebdige, *Subculture*, p. 114.

63 *Ibid.*, p. 98.

64 Cf. Zygmunt Bauman, 'Consuming Life', *Journal of Consumer Culture*, I/1 (2001), p. 25.

65 Cf. *ibid.*, p. 17.

66 *Ibid.*, p. 9.

67 Cf. Diana Crane, *Fashion and its Social Agendas: Class, Gender and Identity in Clothing* (Chicago, 2000), p. 209.

68 Cf. Bauman, 'Consuming Life', pp. 12–13.

69 In this sense, the theory of classical capitalism has been realized as a moral norm. Bernard Mandeville categorized luxury consumption as a 'private vice', but was of the opinion that it contributed to the public good and as such was a public virtue. Adam Smith, on the other hand, thought that Mandeville was too strict towards luxury consumption, claiming that it was fully virtuous from both a private and public perspective.

70 Adorno: 'Om kategoriene statikk og dynamikk i sosiologien', in *Essays i utvalg*, ed. Kjell Eyvind Johansen and Nils Johan Ringdai (Oslo, 1976), p. 97.

71 Baudrillard, *The Consumer Society*, pp. 74–5.

72 *Ibid.*, p. 78.

73 Cf. Bauman, 'Consuming Life', p. 13.

74 Cf. Baudrillard, *The System of Objects*, p. 204.

75 Aristotle, *Nicomachean Ethics*, I.

76 Happiness is undeniably difficult to measure. We can at least state that there is no demonstrable connection between people's level of income and their satisfaction with life. See Robert Lane, *The Market Experience* (Cambridge, 1991), pp. 451–2 and 527–33, for an overview of part of the empiricism in the field.

77 Cf. Bauman, 'Consuming Life'.

78 Cf. Zygmunt Bauman, *Postmodernity and its Discontents* (Cambridge, 1997), p. 40.

8
Fashion as an Ideal in Life

1 Bret Easton Ellis, *American Psycho* (New York, 1991).

2 William Shakespeare, *Hamlet* I.iii.

3 William Hazlitt, 'On the Clerical Character', *Political Essays* (London, 1819).

4 Epictetus, *Discourses* (*c.* AD 105).

5 For a most readable account of the genesis of the modern

self, see Charles Taylor, *Sources of the Self: The Making of Modern Identity* (Cambridge, MA, 1989).

6 Cf. Norbert Elias, *Über den Prozess der Zivilisation: Sosiogenetische und psychogenetische Untersuchungen*, I (Frankfurt am Main, 1997), pp. 51–2.

7 Concerning the concept of lifestyle, see David Chaney, *Lifestyles* (London, 1996), and Anthony Giddens, *Modernity and Self-Identity: Self and Identity in the Late Modern Age* (Cambridge, 1991), pp. 80–87.

8 Anthony Giddens, *New Rules of Sociological Method* (London, 1976), p. 114.

9 Giddens, *Modernity and Self-Identity*, p. 5.

10 Anthony Giddens, *The Transformations of Intimacy* (Oxford, 1992), p. 30.

11 Cf. Pierre Bourdieu, *Le sens pratique* (Paris, 1980; Eng. trans. as *The Logic of Practice*, Cambridge, 1990), pp. 55–6.

12 'Habitus' is also a Latin translation of the Greek 'hexis', and Bourdieu refers in several places to 'hexis'. For Aristotle's concept of 'hexis', see Aristotle, *Nicomachean Ethics*, II, chapters 1, 5 and 6.

13 We can note here that Hegel refers to habit as a 'second nature', i.e. something learned that has been so strongly internalized that it functions as if it was natural (G.W.F. Hegel, *Enzyklopädie der philosophischen Wissenschaften I*, Frankfurt am Main, 1986, p. 410).

14 Pierre Bourdieu, *La distinction: Critique sociale du jugement* (Paris, 1979); trans. Richard Nice (Cambridge, MA, 1984), p. 466.

15 Pierre Bourdieu, *Outline of a Theory of Practice* (Cambridge, 1977), p. 94.

16 Paul Sweetman, 'Twenty-first Century Dis-ease? Habitual Reflexivity or the Reflexive Habitus', *Sociological Review* (2003), p. 537. See also Nick Crossley, *The Social Body: Habit, Identity and Desire* (London, 2001), pp. 117–18, 137–8, 149–50 for an argument that habitus must be reconcilable with reflexivity.

17 'The principle behind the most important differences when it comes to lifestyle, or even more so when it comes to the "stylization of life", lies in differences in the objective and subjective distance from the world, from the material coercion and temporal demands of the world.' Bourdieu, *La distinction*, p. 376.

18 Quoted from Naomi Klein, *No Logo* (London, 2000), p. 23.

19 Quoted from Jennifer Craik, *The Face of Fashion: Cultural Studies in Fashion* (London, 1994), p. 58.

20 Susan Sontag, *On Photography* (Harmondsworth, 1979), p. 153.

21 *Ibid.*, p. 24.

22 Hal Foster, *The Return of the Real: The Avant Garde at the End of the Century* (Cambridge, MA, 1996), p. 83.

23 Hannah Arendt, *The Human Condition* (Chicago and London, 1958), pp. 95–6.

24 Gilles Lipovetsky, *The Empire of Fashion: Dressing Modern Democracy*, ed. Catherine Porter (Princeton, NJ, 1994), p. 149.

25 Friedrich Nietzsche, *Kritische Studienausgabe*, II: *Die fröhliche Wissenschaft* (Munich, 1988), p. 270 [cf. p. 335].

26 *Ibid.*, p. 290.

27 *Ibid.*, p. 107.

28 Michel Foucault, 'On the Genealogy of Ethics', in *Essential Works of Michel Foucault, 1954–1984*, I: *Ethics: Subjectivity and Truth* (New York, 1997), p. 262.

29 See, for example, Michel Foucault, *Discipline and Punish: The Birth of the Prison* (Harmondsworth, 1991).

30 For the concept of asceticism see, for example, Michel Foucault, *The History of Sexuality*, II: *The Use of Pleasure* (Harmondsworth, 1988).

31 Michel Foucault, 'Interview with Michel Foucault', in *Essential Works of Michel Foucault, 1954–1984*, III: *Power* (New York, 2000), pp. 241–2.

32 Michel Foucault, 'Friendship as a Way of Life', in *Ethics: Subjectivity and Truth*, pp. 137–8.

33 Michel Foucault, 'What is Enlightenment?', in *Ethics:*

Subjectivity and Truth.

34 Thomas Carlyle, *Sartor Resartus* (Boston, MA, 1836; repr. Oxford, 1987), p. 207.

35 Oscar Wilde, 'Phrases and Philosophies for the Use of the Young', in *Complete Works of Oscar Wilde* (London, 1966), p. 1206.

36 Quoted from Elisabeth Wilson, *Adorned in Dreams: Fashion and Modernity* (2nd edn, London, 2003), p. 180.

37 Baudelaire, 'The Painter of Modern Life', p. 9.

38 Cf. Dieter Baacke: 'Wechselnde Moden: Stichwörter zur Aneignung eines Mediums durch die Jugend', in *Jugend und Mode: Kleidung als Selbstinzenierung* (Opladen, 1988), p. 25.

39 Oscar Wilde: *De profundis*, in *Complete Works of Oscar Wilde* (London 1966), pp. 874, 896, 900, 916, 953.

40 *Ibid.*, p. 934.

41 *Ibid.*, p. 926.

42 Cf. *Ibid.*, p. 916.

43 Taylor, *Sources of the Self*, p. 14.

44 *Ibid.*, pp. 16–23, 25–49.

45 *Ibid.*, p. 43.

46 Lipovetsky, *The Empire of Fashion*, p. 149.

47 Holly Brubach, *A Dedicated Follower of Fashion* (London, 1999), p. 15.

48 See, for example, Douglas Kellner, 'Madonna, Fashion, and Identity', in *On Fashion*, ed. Shari Benstock and Suzanne Ferris (New Brunswick, NJ, 1994),

49 See the essays on personal and narrative identity and the self and narrative identity in Paul Ricoeur, *Eksistens og Hermeneutikk* (Oslo, 1999). See also Alasdair MacIntyre, *After Virtue* (London, 1981, 2/1984), particularly pp. 204–25, for a perspective related to that of Ricoeur.

50 This self is threatened not only as a consumer but also as a producer. Richard Sennett underlines that work in postmodern capitalism creates an experience of time that undermines man's ability to tell cohesive narratives about himself (Richard

Sennett, *The Corrosion of Character: The Personal Consequences of Work in the New Capitalism*, New York, 1988, p. 31).

51 Søren Kierkegaard, *Enten-Eller. Anden Deel, Samlede Verker*, vol. III (Copenhagen, 1962)

52 *Ibid.*, p. 184.

53 Kierkegaard, *Gentagelsen, Samlede Verker*, vol. III (Copenhagen, 1962), p. 131.

54 Virginia Woolf, *Orlando* (London, 1928, repr. Harmondsworth, 1990), p. 108.

55 Colin McDowell, ed., *The Pimlico Companion to Fashion: A Literary Anthology* (London, 1998), pp. 407–8.

56 'One can no more escape fashion than one can flee time, because fashion is the indelible mark of our temporality' (Mark C. Taylor, *Hiding*, Chicago, 1997, p. 125).

57 Georg Simmel, *Gesamtausgabe*, X: *Philosophie der Mode* (Frankfurt am Main, 1989), pp. 20–21.

58 Lipovetsky, *The Empire of Fashion*, p. 29.

59 *Ibid.*, p. 37.

60 *Ibid.*, p. 206.

61 *Ibid.*, pp. 102ff.

62 Martha C. Nussbaum, 'Sex, Virtue and the Costumes of the Middle Class', *New Republic*, 2 January 1995.

63 It must be admitted that Lipovetsky does not exclusively paint a rosy picture of fashion. He claims for example that fashion 'tempers social conflicts, but deepens subjective and intersubjective conflicts'. Lipovetsky, *The Empire of Fashion*, p. 241.

64 Broch: *Hofmansthal og hans tid*, ed. Sverre Dahl (Oslo, 1987), p. 69.

65 Taylor, *Sources of the Self*, pp. 30, 34.

66 The classic formulation of the distinction between negative and positive freedom is given by Isaiah Berlin in *Four Essays on Liberty* (Oxford, 1969).

Conclusion

1 Weeping Willows, 'Touch Me', *Into the Light* (2002), Virgin 8117592
2 This is due not least to the decline in tourism on a world basis (which in turn is due to the fear of terrorism, SARS virus, etc.), since tourists account for a quarter of all luxury purchases. Prada is struggling with a debt of several millions, Gucci is making a loss, Versace has more than halved the number of its shops, and the value of the company has dropped by almost 40 per cent since 1997. Even though a number of the big fashion houses are struggling, this does not mean that people have stopped buying clothes, and it is a market that constantly recruits new participants. Consumption of clothes in Norway increased by 30 per cent in the course of the 1990s (see Erling Dokk Holm, *Fra Gud til Gucci*, Oslo, 2004).
3 *The Economist*, 4 March 2004.
4 Baudelaire describes a contemporary art exhibition as 'full of confusion, a jumble of styles and colours, a cacophony of tones, enormous trivialities, a vulgarity of gestures and attitudes, a conventional exclusiveness, every type of cliché; and all of this presents itself clearly and strikingly, not only in the combination of pictures, but even in the same picture: in short, a complete absence of anything unifying; and the result is terribly tiring for the spirit and the eyes.' Baudelaire, *The Painter of Modern Life and Other Essays* (London, 1964). That could have been a relatively sober description of today's fashion.
5 Georg Simmel: 'Die Krisis der Kultur', in *Gesamtausgabe*, XIII (Frankfurt am Main, 1989), p. 197.
6 Anne Hollander, *Seeing through Clothes* (Berkeley, CA, 1975, rev. 1993), p. 345.
7 Malcolm McLaren: 'Hyper-Allergic', in *The Penguin Book of Twentieth-Century Fashion Writing*, ed. Judith Watt

(Harmondsworth, 1999), pp. 222–3.

8 In conclusion one can ask who this 'we' is that so often occurs in this text. 'We' who have come increasingly under the dominance of fashion. 'We' are apparently not everyone, but 'we' consist of more than a handful of people. 'We' is an idealized entity, a generalization or an ideal type, if you prefer, that gives a picture of a kind of subject that has emerged over a long period of time, several centuries, and of whom there are more and more. It is a subject detached from all traditions and that is referred to having to construct an identity out of the bricks that the late capitalist world can offer, where external signs – not least in the form of brand names – are central. Against this, one can object that 'most people' are not like that yet, but 'most people' are not what they were. More and more 'most people' become like this 'we' that has figured in the text – and there is a host of consumer research that supports such an assertion (see, for example, chapter Seven, n. 5 above). It must be conceded that 'most people' does not yet completely coincide with 'we', but there is reason to fear that one day that may be the case.

9 Caroline Evans, *Fashion at the Edge: Spectacle, Modernity and Deathliness* (New Haven, CT, 2003), p. 19.